Bar Exam Mind

A strategy guide for an anxiety-free bar exam

MATT RACINE

DEDICATION

To Jenny, Luke, and Mia:
You guys are the best.

CONTENTS

INTRODUCTION

In most states, the bar examination is a feared obstacle for all those who want to be lawyers.

The bar exam strikes terror into the hearts of third-year law students and has laid low takers who graduated first in their law school class, who graduated from top-tier law schools, and even those who have been practicing law for many years and must take the examination again when they move to another state. During administrations of the exam, test takers have been known to faint, suffer panic attacks, or vomit. The stress level is intense; the psychic and financial price of failure is high.

It does not have to be that way.

I have passed two bar examinations: Oregon (July 2006) and California (February 2008). Pass rates for the Oregon exam are usually between 70% and 80%, while the pass rate for the California exam hovers around 50%, and is often lower (e.g., the examination that I passed had an overall pass rate of just under 40%). I passed both tests on my first attempt. Did I enroll in some magical test-preparation course that creates 100% pass-rates? No. Do I have a photographic memory? No. Did I cheat? Of course not.

Over the past few years I have been writing a blog about the bar examination called Bar Advisor. The blog contains advice on how to study and how to approach various sections of the bar exam. This is very useful information. Still, the more posts that I added to the blog, the more I realized that there is a single fundamental building block upon which all bar exam success rests:

You must have a Bar Exam Mind.

Those who believe will achieve. You cannot go into the final weeks of the preparation period before the bar exam thinking that you will or even might fail. You need to resolve the issue of failure early in your preparations and move past it. Nor can you afford to spend your mental and physical energy dealing with stress and worry. You must learn techniques to free yourself from these fatiguing and distracting mental states.

Get to the point where preparation and practice, rather than your psychic preoccupations, are the only things that matter. If you cannot move past fear, anxiety, worry, and stress, your preparations will be handicapped, perhaps to the point where you will not be able to prepare sufficiently to tackle the bar exam.

My new blog (Bar Exam Mind at www.barexammind.com) and this book are dedicated to helping you create your own Bar Exam Mind.

◇◇◇◇◇

When most people (and I was no exception) first begin studying for the bar exam, the magnitude of the information that you need to learn is so overwhelming that it is easy to become highly stressed. In fact, it is understandable that some form of panic *initially* sets in.

The important thing is to realize in the midst of this panic is that hundreds of thousands (millions?) of people have passed the bar exam. Most of them are very ordinary people. You can do this.

The goal of this book is to teach you techniques and strategies to create a Bar Exam Mind to enable you to approach studying for the bar exam calmly. When we learn in a state of calm, we are more focused and can learn and retain information more quickly and more thoroughly than if we are learning while trapped in a state of anxiety.

As you work through the exercises in this book and begin developing and strengthening your Bar Exam Mind, your stress level will decrease the closer you get to the bar exam.

Peak performance and peak learning occur during periods of extreme focus and pure acceptance of what you are experiencing. I am not saying that you need to get into some New Age trance in order to pass the bar exam. I am saying that you cannot fight against the hours and hours of review and memorization of substantive, black-letter law necessary to pass the bar exam.

You cannot view bar exam study as drudgery or a form of punishment. It is simply the needed means to achieve a goal that *you* have set for *yourself*:

Own your choices.

The benefits of such an outlook are, at least, three-fold: (1) learning is much easier when you are enjoying yourself (or at least you are not constantly whispering to yourself, "this sucks"); (2) it is much easier to recall information learned while in a positive, focused mental state; and (3) when learning is easier, you can complete your studies in less time and have more time for friends and family, thus decreasing the feeling of drudgery weeks of study can induce in the mind and soul.

I have written on the Bar Advisor blog that overall success on the bar exam boils down to three things: (1) diligence; (2) anticipation of conditions; and (3) stress reduction.

- Diligence is simply the requirement that you prepare continuously and systematically for the examination without interruption or distraction. (This is something to be done in discrete, highly-focused, and *limited* periods, not 24/7 for ten weeks.)
- Anticipation of conditions is the need to understand how the test is administered and to practice under test-like conditions.
- Stress reduction involves the mediation of anxiety and fear so that these negative mental and emotional states do not interfere with maximum preparation and

performance. In short, practice well and often, and be ready and willing to take what the bar exam gives you.

Within those three broad categories, this book explains techniques and strategies that will enable you to create the proper mental outlook for your review of substantive law and for your successful completion of the bar exam.

To that end, this book focuses on three important techniques to develop your mental and emotional well-being in the face of the bar exam: stress-reduction through visualization and affirmations, self-understanding through journaling, and anticipation of conditions through a variety of methods. In addition, this book details proper nutrition and supplementation to allow your brain to perform at optimal levels.

Visualization

Visualization is the mental picturing of an outcome or situation for the purpose of both learning from the envisioned outcome or situation and learning to influence that outcome or situation. There are two types of visualization: positive and negative. I will show you how to use both forms of visualization to assist you in passing the bar exam.

Positive visualization is used to picture a *desired* outcome or goal as if that outcome or goal has already come to pass. For example, you have probably seen athletes with their eyes closed before competition, visualizing what they plan to do when it is their turn to compete. By so visualizing, the athlete convinces herself that she has already successfully completed the competition. Now, her body movements need to make it a reality. The athlete's thoughts have actually affected the outcome of her performance in the physical world. Through a series of visualization exercises in this book, you will use your imagination to prepare yourself to perform at peak levels and to create the desired outcome of bar exam passage.

Negative visualization is the process of visualizing an *undesired* outcome in realistic detail and then analyzing what can be done to avoid the outcome or to recover from it. Negative visualization is especially helpful in the reduction of fear and anxiety. In Chapter One, I will set out a negative visualization exercise that is crucial for you to perform at the beginning of you bar exam preparations. An honest and complete use of this negative visualization will assist hugely in calming you for your bar exam experience. This exercise is fundamental in the creation of a Bar Exam Mind.

Affirmations

Affirmations are short, strong, and positive statements used to train your mind to believe you can achieve your goals and aspirations. An affirmation is an affirmative statement that something has *already* come to pass. For example, if your goal is to lose weight, you might use the affirmation, "I am fit and attractive" or "I love having a healthy and fit body."

Affirmations may be recited silently, spoken aloud, or written down. The important thing with affirmations is repetition. By repeating a *positive* affirmation, we crowd out any *negative* thoughts from our mind that might be preventing us from achieving our goals.

In many ways, affirmations are like short visualizations. In fact, a typical way to use affirmations is to say them before and after a visualization exercise. This book provides you with affirmations to use during your bar exam preparation and teaches you how to make your own powerful affirmations.

Journaling

Journaling is the systematic recordation of your thoughts and emotional responses to those thoughts. By creating a record of your thoughts and emotions related to the bar exam, you will be able to prevent anxieties and worries from become debilitating. When you bring these anxieties into the light of day they cannot hide in the shadows, menacing you.

The basic idea behind journaling as discussed in this book is that you will filter your emotions and thoughts about the bar exam through objects of contemplation (i.e., a topic, quote, or question). In response to each object of contemplation, you will write whatever pops into your head. By so doing, you will cleanse your mind of whatever it is that has been troubling you – whether consciously or unconsciously – that day. If you had anxieties, they will be lessened; if you were over-confident, it will be tempered. After the journaling exercise, you will be able to see the progress of your test preparation more clearly.

Journaling is especially important to those who feel they do not have anyone to talk to about the bar exam. The process of journaling can lessen your feelings of isolation because the cathartic act of expressing your feelings in response to an object of contemplation is a form of dialogue. Unlike the Socratic Method as it is normally misused in law schools, the trajectory of the journaling dialogue is entirely under your control.

In this book, I have incorporated journaling into the 21-day schedule for you. Most of the days set aside for journaling incorporate a topic, question, or quote for you to contemplate and write about. There are also days for free writing. Free writing is important because it is typically during an extended free writing session that our greatest fears or our greatest strengths are pushed to the forefront of our thoughts. To build and strengthen your Bar Exam Mind, it is important to be aware of both of these aspects of the self.

Anticipation of Conditions

In order to succeed on the bar examination – or any important test of mental or intellectual ability – one must prepare for it under conditions approximating that "test" situation. This is why people in the military have live-fire exercises and combat training. You don't just hand someone a gun, drop him off in enemy territory, and say, "Go to it." While failure on the bar exam has much less drastic consequences than failure in a war zone, there are lessons to be learned from the intense and cinematic preparation that an advanced military undertakes.

The bar exam is, for most people, a highly stressed two- or three-day period. For some takers, it may be the most stressful situation they have ever been in. Therefore, understanding what the test will be like and practicing under similar conditions is of utmost importance for keeping that stress to a minimum.

There are two central aspects of the bar exam for which one must prepare: 1) performing at a high level for 6-8 hours for two or three days in a row and 2) performing while surrounded by hundreds or even thousands of people who are frantically taking the same test you are.

This book shows you how to practice in test-like environments and how to use visualization techniques to prepare for different sections of the bar exam.

Nutrition

In addition to these techniques for training your mind to perform well under the strain of bar exam preparation, this book discusses nutrition, diet and supplements, with the aim of improving the physical structure and functioning of your brain during this crucial period. After all, if your physical brain is not in top shape, then all the mental gymnastics in the world may not have the desired effect.

This book discusses supplements that are recommended by medical professionals to assist with your ability to focus, to relax, and to get healthy sleep. These three abilities are interrelated. If you can focus well while studying and relax fully when not studying, then you should be able to sleep well. If one or more of these three things is missing, you may need some supplementation to get back on track.

Conclusion

Anyone studying for the bar exam – or even thinking about studying for the exam – knows that it is stressful. Through the use of visualization, affirmations, journaling, practicing under exam-like conditions, and proper nutrition, you will build a Bar Exam Mind able to put the stress of studying for the bar exam in its proper perspective, and not let it destroy the ability of your mind to learn the necessary material. By creating a Bar Exam Mind, you will perform well on the bar exam.

Let's get started.

21-DAY STUDY SCHEDULE

This book is designed so that you can learn and gain initial mastery of all of its techniques and strategies in 21 days, with an average time commitment of 20 minutes per day (with the exception of the first few days).

(If you don't have 21 days or don't want to follow the schedule, skip to the end of this schedule for some other suggestions about how to make the most of this book.)

◈ ◈ ◈

Day 1:   Read the Introduction and Chapter One: "Visualize Your Fears"

Day 2:   Return to Chapter One and go through the steps of the "Stoic Method" for dealing with bar exam fears. Take as much time as you need to perform this task.

Day 3: Return to Chapter One and use the "Clearing Method" for cleansing yourself of bar exam fears. Take as much time as you need to perform this task.

Day 4: Read Chapter Two: "Visualize Your Success" and perform visualization script 1: "Studying well and learning and retaining knowledge". Modify the script as necessary to make it as meaningful as possible to you.

Day 5: Read Chapter Three: "Affirmations" and perform the written exercise discussed in the chapter.

Day 6: Read Chapter Four: "Start Your Journal" and perform Exercise One.

Day 7: Read Chapter Five: "Nutrition for Learning and Focus." Determine what nutritional and lifestyle changes you need to make to improve the functioning of your brain and to alleviate stress and anxiety.

Day 8: Read Chapter Six: "Anticipation of Conditions." Determine when you will be able to do a "full-blown" practice test as described in the chapter. Determine how you will incorporate practice testing into your study schedule.

Then, return to Chapter Two and perform visualization script 2: "Walking into the bar exam testing room and remaining calm." Modify the script as necessary to make it as meaningful as possible to you.

Day 9: Return to Chapter Four and perform journaling Exercise Two.

Day 10: Return to Chapter Three. Review the section about writing your own affirmations. Create at least two affirmations you can recite to yourself each morning when you wake up and each evening when you go to sleep. Incorporate the recitation of these affirmations into your daily routine.

Day 11: Return to Chapter Two and perform visualization scripts 3 and 4: "Writing a great essay" and "Writing a great performance test." Modify the scripts as necessary to make them as meaningful as possible to you.

Day 12: Return to Chapter Four and perform journaling Exercise Three

Day 13: Return to Chapter Two and perform visualization script 5: "Doing well on the MBE." Modify the script as necessary to make it as meaningful as possible to you.

Day 14: Read through all of your journal entries to date. What trends are you noticing? Are there any recurring themes? Are there any fears or anxieties cropping up that you need to deal with using negative visualization? If so, review the negative visualization techniques in Chapter One and take action. You may also wish to create your own visualization script(s) to address these issues.

Day 15: Return to Chapter Two and perform visualization scripts 6 and 7: "Receiving your passing results" and "Attending the swearing-in ceremony." Modify these scripts as necessary to make them as meaningful as possible to you.

Day 16: Review the nutritional and lifestyle changes you incorporated after Day 7. Are they making a difference? Review Chapter Five to determine if you need to make any adjustments to your nutritional and supplementation program.

Day 17: Go to Appendix D. Fill-in and sign the "bar exam passage" contract. (If you don't want to write in your book, use the web link in the appendix to get an electronic version of the contract.) Then, write out at least 30 times each of the affirmations you created on Day 10.

Day 18: Return to Chapter One and perform visualization scripts 1 and 2. Then, go to Appendix A. Read the instructions then select two quotes that seem relevant and interesting. Write journal responses to both quotes.

Day 19: Sit quietly, take a few minutes to enter a state of deep relaxation, then contemplate the progress of your bar exam studies. What is coming easily to you and what has been more difficult? Next, return to Chapter One and perform visualization scripts 3, 4, and 5.

Day 20: Review Chapter Six. Have you been incorporating its suggestions for training your mind and body to endure the rigors of a multi-day test? If yes, write a journal entry about how you have incorporated these techniques and what their effect has been on your studies. If no, determine how you will implement these techniques during the time you have left before the exam.

Day 21: Return to Chapter Four and perform journaling Exercise Four. Then, return to Chapter One and perform visualization scripts 6 and 7.

CONGRATULATIONS! You have completed the Bar Exam Mind program. But, this does not mean you should stop using the information you have learned in this book.

In the remaining days before the bar exam, continue to use the techniques that you feel have been most useful to you. At the very least, I recommend continuing with positive visualization and journaling.

◇ ◇ ◇

Don't want to spend 21 days on this program or don't have 21 days until the bar exam? Then do this:

- Read Chapter One, and perform the negative visualization exercises to rid yourself of bar-exam-related fear. Once you have completed the negative visualization exercise, read straight through the remainder of the book.

- Incorporate positive visualization and affirmations into your study schedule as often as possible.

- Incorporate all of the journaling exercises in Chapter Four into your bar exam studies, ideally completing them at least two weeks before the exam. After that, write in your journal as often as possible, using the "Quote Grab Bag" in Appendix A as inspiration when needed.

- Determine which, if any, of the diet and nutritional suggestions you might incorporate into your studies.

- Finally, use the suggestions in Chapter Six to prepare your mind and body for the rigors of the bar exam testing schedule.

Good luck!

CHAPTER ONE
VISUALIZE YOUR FEARS

"How does one kill fear, I wonder? How do you shoot a spectre through the heart, slash off its spectral head, take it by its spectral throat?"

– Joseph Conrad, *Lord Jim*

"Where fear is, happiness is not."

– Seneca, *Letters to Lucilius*

"A matter that becomes clear ceases to concern us."

– Nietzsche, *Beyond Good and Evil*

As I noted in the Introduction, there are two types of visualization: negative and positive. In this chapter, I will discuss two techniques of negative visualization that you can use to rid yourself of that most pernicious of fears of the bar examinee: fear of failing the bar exam.

Whether one is a first-time taker or a repeater, most people preparing for the bar exam are afraid of what will happen if they fail. They are afraid while they study, they are afraid while they are taking the actual test, and they are most afraid while they await the release of bar exam results. You must do all you can to approach the bar exam in a fearless state because when you are in a fearful or anxious state, you often attract the situations or results that you want to avoid.

The Danger of Fear

In *The Power of Now*, Eckhart Tolle speaks of an "anxiety gap." He argues that fear is separate and apart from any real immediate danger. Fear can come in many forms, such as anxiety, nervousness, dread, phobia, or tension. Psychological fear is always about some suspected consequence, rather than about something that is actually happening to you.

For example, if you worry about being attacked by a shark, that is fear, but if you are actually being attacked by a shark, you are no longer fearful, you are reacting to the attack. This worry about an uncertain future occurrence creates the anxiety gap. Where there is an anxiety gap, you worry about the future while living in the present at the cost of your ability to focus on and be present in the now.

Furthermore, if we act in a state of fear, that state exerts a strong influence on our reality. If we act out of fear or in response to fear, it is much more likely that what we fear will come to pass. Therefore, it is important to confront fear early in the process of bar exam preparation so that its influence can be removed.

This chapter is about two different methods to rid yourself of bar exam-related fears and to destroy the "anxiety gap" so that you can focus on your studies without stultifying worry. Indeed, the first thing we must do in dealing with any challenge, such as the bar exam, is to acknowledge the challenge and determine how we feel about the challenge. By facing our fears and concerns about the upcoming challenge, we can find effective solutions.

The first method for removing fear arises from the Stoic philosopher Seneca, and is likely to resonate most with people who are very logical and concrete in their thinking. The second method is called "clearing" and is most likely to be effective for people who are more emotional in their thinking about fear.

My own fear

Before we get to the actual techniques to remove fear, let me tell you about my own bar exam fears. See if any of this sounds familiar to you.

I was afraid of failing the bar exam both of the times that I took it: in Oregon and in California. I was afraid of failing the Oregon bar examination because I had never taken a bar exam before, so it was an unknown quantity to me. I had never failed a major test in my life (though came close to it when I took my driving test when I was 16), and so the possibility of failing one of the most important tests of my life was a *huge* source of fear. Still, I knew that a substantial majority of people who took the Oregon bar exam passed (70% on average in most years), and because I did well in law school, I figured that I could perform well enough on the test to be among the group of passers. Despite these encouraging facts, I was fearful until I received the news that I had indeed passed.

My fear during the California bar exam was of a different variety. Because the Oregon bar exam was similar to the California exam, though a day shorter in duration, I was not afraid of failing the California bar due to my lack of familiarity with the bar examination process itself. In fact, I knew that if I studied conscientiously, I *should* pass the exam, assuming no rogue grader took a dislike to my writing style and failed me for aesthetic reasons. My fear arose from worry about the *consequences* of failure.

It is clear to me that fear truly is about how we view the consequences of a result rather than the result itself. Indeed, a result is merely a fact with no meaning other than what we give to it. Therefore, to remove fear of the consequences of failure, we must examine the consequences that we fear and do away with those fears in one way or another. Once our fear of adverse consequences is gone, there is no reason not to do something and do it well.

Let me set up the situation I was in when I began preparing for the California bar exam. My wife, two children, and I had just relocated from Oregon back to our hometown. We were burning through savings and imposing on the hospitality of relatives. We had some other pretty heavy things going on in our lives relating to the health of a close relative. If I failed, what would we do for money? How would I get a job? What would happen to all of our dreams and goals? Would law school end up being a waste of three years and tens of thousands of dollars?

The following methods are designed to allay precisely these sorts of fears and give you peace of mind needed to be able to focus on your bar exam studies rather than your anxieties. Be sure to read both sections and try both techniques. If one seems to work better than the other, then stick with it. Otherwise, I suggest alternating between these techniques as necessary.

Method one: Stoic method

The Stoic technique[1] for achieving peace of mind has to do with understanding the consequences of results that you fear. The basic technique is: define down to the smallest detail all the worst case scenarios, list all of the things you could do to minimize the worst case scenarios from happening, and then define how you will recover if any of these scenarios come to pass.

This technique is devilishly simple, but to be effective, the definitions and lists must be thorough and precise. Thus, this technique involves real, intense effort.

---

[1] This technique first came to my attention while reading *The 4-Hour Workweek*, by Timothy Ferriss.

The first step in this method is negative visualization, which is where you define your feared consequences (your worst case scenarios) rather than your goals. The first part of negative visualization is writing out a list of all feared consequences of failing the bar exam.

To do this exercise correctly, you need to list *all* the real and imagined consequences of bar exam failure. For example, my list at the time I was preparing for the California bar exam would probably have looked something like this (keep in mind these are *worst case* scenarios; some of which are far-fetched, but then, most fears are):

- My wife will think I am a loser and leave me.
- My in-laws will think I am a loser.
- My parents will think I am a loser.
- My friends from law school will pity me publicly and laugh about me privately.
- I will never be able to get a job.
- I'll go insane.
- I will become suicidal.
- I'll have to get a low-paying, thankless job and all my money will go to rent and law school debt.
- I'll be a wage slave the rest of my life.
- My children will starve.
- I'll have to take this damn test over and over again.
- I'll never be able to own a house.
- Etc.

There is no minimum or maximum length for this list. Just make sure that you spend enough time working through your feared consequences so that you get every last one of them written down. Of course, each item in your list should be expanded into as much detail as possible so that each feared consequence is fully explored.

In order to ensure that you have sufficient detail, take some time to contemplate deeply each of these feared consequences. Visualize each consequence coming to pass and inhabit it fully – intellectually and emotionally – for a moment. Get the full sense of what each one of these consequences will mean for your life.

I note here that this technique may draw up some deep, powerful emotions. You may want to perform this exercise where you can have privacy the entire time. Honesty is critical for this exercise, and honesty can sometimes be painful.

If done properly and if you have a long list of fears, this exercise could take many hours. That is ok.

The second step is to determine all the things you can do to minimize your customized list of horribles from coming to pass. My pre-bar exam list of ways to minimize my feared consequences might have looked like this:

- Commit to focused studying without distractions; if this means leaving my cell phone and other gadgets in my car when I go to the library, so be it.
- Follow my study schedule and crush it while I am in the library during my designated study time.
- Talk to wife about my fears and tell her of the possibility of failure.
- Talk to parents and in-laws about difficulty in passing the bar exam. (This sets up their admiration if I pass

but makes it more acceptable to them that I failed such a daunting test.)

- Get in contact with as many friends and acquaintances as possible, and let them know that I am interested in any jobs they know about, just in case I don't pass the bar exam. If they can vouch for me, it is less likely an employer will think that I will re-take the bar exam (even though I will . . .), which makes finding a non-law job so difficult.
- Review prior plans for starting a business; maybe the business is viable in the event of bar failure.
- Etc.

The final (and, in my opinion, most important) step in the Stoic Method is to create a resolution chart listing the concrete steps you will take to *recover* (financially, mentally, emotionally) if any of your list of feared consequences comes to pass. In other words, how will you return to the pre-bar exam status quo?

My resolution chart would have looked something like this:

Consequence #1

Suicidal Thoughts

Resolution #1

Call primary care physician for a referral to a psychiatrist. Don't worry that most of my family thinks therapy is stupid. This is about survival.

Consequence #2

Low-Paying Job

Resolution #2

Take any job I can get, but also update LinkedIn to reflect prior successes and jobs. Reads books and blogs about how to land a job outside of the legal field. Revive plans for on-line business that I scrapped during law school.

Consequence #3

Kids will Starve

Resolution #3

Talk to friends and relatives about sharing purchases of bulk food items. Find a way to plant a garden. Apply for food stamps if I qualify.

Etc.

In the end, you should have resolved all of your feared consequences such that you do not need to think about them anymore. Should one come to pass, consult your resolution chart and act as planned.

Should a new fear or feared consequence arise during the course of your bar exam studies, take that new fear and process it through the three steps already discussed.

Once your feared consequences have been studied fully and processed completely through these three steps, your mind if free to focus on the task at hand: Learning the information and practicing the techniques necessary to pass the bar exam.

Method two: Clearing the Fear

The basic idea behind clearing[2] is that all of us have certain "blocks" in our thinking that keep us from achieving our highest good and greatest success. Clearing is used to remove those blocks. As applicable here, the block we are talking about is fear, and particularly fear of failure.

How do we remove that block?

First, we need to understand more deeply what a "block" really is. A block is something that prevents our energy from moving on a particular path. Thus, the fear of failing the bar exam acts to prevent the energy needed for passing the exam to flow to the places where it is needed to make bar passage a reality. Therefore, your goal in using clearing is to remove the fear block and permit your energy to flow where it is needed to allow you to achieve your goal of passing the bar exam.

---

[2] I first learned about clearing while reading *Creative Visualization*, by Shakti Gawain.

The steps to clearing a block are actually similar to the Stoic method discussed above, though the steps are focused on internal observation rather than on external list-making. Clearing should be done where you can relax. Therefore, find a quiet spot where you can be alone and undisturbed for at least one hour.

Once you are comfortable, the first step is to accept, both mentally and emotionally, the fact that you are afraid of failing the bar exam. You cannot sweep this feeling under the rug or ignore it, but must truly feel the emotion. Embrace this fact for as long as it takes to fully comprehend it. Once you have felt the emotion of fear fully, you will, paradoxically, relax physically. Acceptance leads to relaxation.

Next, you need to honestly and keenly observe what is root of the fear. This is not as simple as saying, "Oh, I will be broke" or "My friends will think I am a loser." There is always more than concern about one's material well-being or one's social standing.

Is there a fear of poverty rooted in something experienced as a child? Do you have a fear of humiliation based on things that family or friends repeatedly said to you when you were younger? Perhaps your fear arises from your own pride and how failure on the bar exam would crush your own self-image? The question to be asking yourself as you observe the root of the fear is: What is the belief(s) *I* hold about *myself* that is allowing this fear to exist?

Sit and observe your fear for as long as it takes for you to see the root cause of the fear. For some, this may only take a few moments; for others, a few hours and maybe even repeated observations will be necessary to arrive at an understanding of the true root of fear.

Once you have determined what belief or beliefs about yourself are creating and sustaining your fear of bar exam failure, you are ready to clear it from your life and unblock your energy for success.

The final step in clearing requires you to accept you hold a belief that created fear in you. Once you accept that it was okay for you to have held this belief, you can then see that it is time for you to let go of the belief because holding on to it is limiting your ability to be successful. You no longer need this belief; say goodbye to it.

Now, the fear block is cleared from your life, and your energy is free to help you pass the bar

Conclusion

Deep examination of fear and feared consequences is much healthier than ignoring or repressing them. When we deny our negative thoughts and concentrate only on positive thoughts, those denied thoughts will bubble to the surface one way or another. If we only focus on positive thoughts, we may actually make our situation worse.

When we attempt to escape from our fear, we feel a sense of helplessness because the fear is always there, pursuing us. When we open ourselves to the source of fear, we can fully understand the source of the fear and the effect the fear has on us.

This is why – ideally before you start studying for the bar exam – you should spend some time exploring any bar exam-related fears you have. This can be difficult, as we are programmed from an early age to withdraw our awareness from unpleasant and discomforting feelings and emotions.

By the act of studying our fear, we turn the fear into an object rather than something that is a part of ourselves. By objectifying the fear, studying it, and arriving at solutions for overcoming the fear (and its consequences), we are more easily able to separate the fear from ourselves. It is no longer "our fear" but merely "the fear." It becomes something we can easily ignore. This is important for having a clear, focused mind while studying for the bar exam. Fear should not impede upon your days of study.

By doing one or both of the exercises discussed in this chapter, you will be able, first, to think more clearly about your fear and, second, to remove any deleterious effects the fear would otherwise have on your ability to study for the bar exam.

The foundation for your Bar Exam Mind is now in place.

CHAPTER TWO
VISUALIZE YOUR SUCCESS

"If thou may not continually gather thyself together, do it some time at least once a day, morning or evening."

    – Thomas à Kempis

"Seeing is believing."

    – Unknown

This chapter deals with the second type of visualization and the one you will be using most often as you create your Bar Exam Mind: positive visualization.

Positive visualization is a technique where you use your imagination to create clear images, ideas, and feelings of something you want to occur in your life. You focus on these images, ideas, and feelings until they become reality and your goal has been met. In other words, you are using your thoughts to affect the outer world. Positive visualization breaks down all internal barriers that might otherwise act as roadblocks on your way to successful passage of the bar exam.

Positive visualization is linked intimately with practicing for the bar exam under test-like conditions, which I discuss in Chapter Six. Visualization and anticipation of exam conditions have a synergistic effect on each other. By visualizing both what we want to accomplish and how we expect to perform, we can influence the conditions under which we study for and take the bar examination.

For the bar exam, you should visualize the most important parts of the bar exam testing process. You will visualize completing these segments calmly and successfully, just as you will do when you are actually performing these tasks. As these visualizations become more clear and certain, their effectiveness increases as well.

In chronological order, the most important parts of the bar exam process are:

(1) Studying well in order to learn and retain knowledge;

(2) Walking into the bar exam testing room and remaining calm;

(3) Writing a great essay;

(4) Writing a great performance test;

(5) Doing well on the MBE;

(6) Receiving your passing results; and

(7) Attending the swearing-in ceremony.

Before you can visualize these situations effectively, you need to learn the proper technique for positive visualization.

How to Visualize

I recommend you perform visualizations either first thing in the morning or last thing in the evening, and if you have time to visualize during the morning *and* the evening, even better! Morning and evening are best because it is during these times that the body and mind are most relaxed, which is important for visualization.

Step 1: Find a quiet place where you can be alone for at least 15 minutes. You can sit in a chair or lie down in bed. When I was studying for the California bar exam, I typically would perform visualizations while lying down in bed after my kids (loud, active 4- and 2-year olds at the time) were asleep. Sometimes, I even fell asleep while visualizing, which I actually think is a good thing because your positive visualization can transfer into your dreams and crowd out the anxiety dreams people often have while preparing for the bar exam.

Step 2: Once you have found the quiet place and time, close your eyes and relax. Do not forget to relax! For a visualization to be successful, it is important to enter a state of deep relaxation. If you already have a relaxation technique that works for you, please use it. If not, try deep, slow breathing for one minute while imagining yourself in your favorite place.

Step 3: When you feel relaxed, it is time to visualize. See and feel the situation you want to occur. Include as much detail as possible: **Live the visualization.** The more real the visualization is, the more effective it is.

I have included visualization scripts for the seven major chronological moments of the bar exam which are listed above. You can stick with the scripts, or use them as a basis for your own visualization. Modification of the scripts is important, especially if details in the scripts (e.g., location of the exam, number of people taking the test, etc.) do not match the situation you know you will encounter on the examination.

There is, however, no need for your visualizations about the bar exam to match the exam situation precisely. Unless you are repeating the bar exam, you will not have the experience to get many of the details exactly right. What matters is that you repeat these visualizations until you *see* and *feel* yourself writing a great essay or *see* yourself attending the swearing-in ceremony and *feeling* the swelling pride having become an attorney.

Visualization Scripts

The scripts below are examples for your use. You can use them verbatim, or modify them as necessary. The point of visualization is not to repeat unhelpful words over and over, but to actually *see* and *feel* yourself engaging with a situation or performing an action in the way you want to do. If these scripts create salient, evocative mental images and emotional responses for you, then stick with them. If not, create your own scripts using these as a guide.

Using visualization scripts

Begin reciting each script only after you have entered into a state of relaxation as discussed earlier in this chapter. Also, please note that the scripts are in the present tense. This is purposeful because your visualizations should be from the point of view of having *already acquired* the skills you seek by performing the visualization.

(1) Studying well and learning and retaining knowledge

I know that in order to pass the bar exam, I will need to study well. I will need to study for many hours and days. There is a lot to learn.

Fortunately, I am able to review the material without feeling overwhelmed. When it seems like I am having trouble learning a concept, I remain calm and take a deep breath. I have plenty of time to learn enough to pass the bar exam. I

35

cannot learn it all in one day, so I maintain a steady, focused study schedule.

During each day of my studies, I wake up and eat a nutritious breakfast. I gather my study materials and go to the library. When I arrive at the library, I put my cell phone on "silent" and I disable my wireless connection on my computer so that I will not be distracted by phone calls, text messages, instant messages, email, or websites.

I begin my task for the day. Whatever it is (review outlines, practice writing essays, practice MBE questions, etc.) I do it in a steady, focused manner. Sometimes I hear people talking and tune into their conversation, but I quickly re-direct my mind to studying. I know that my success on the bar exam is tied to my ability to focus while I study.

As I study, I feel myself learning and retaining the knowledge necessary to pass the bar exam. I am learning all of the elements of torts, the tests for the various levels of judicial scrutiny, the rules of evidence, and everything else.

Some days studying are boring, but it must be done. I chose this path for myself, and I will complete it. On the rare moments when I cannot seem to focus on studying, I get up and go outside to walk around and think about something other than the law. I give my mind a break for a few minutes. When I return to the library, I am refreshed and ready to continue studying.

By staying on my study schedule I am able to learn and review every topic for the bar exam. It is amazing that I am able to retain all of this information in my mind at once, but I am able to do it. In fact, it becomes easier everyday to retain this information.

I am proud of myself and look forward to taking the exam.

(2) Walking into the bar exam testing room and remaining calm

On the morning of the bar exam, I wake up in my hotel room refreshed from a night of restful sleep. After I wake up, I get dressed, eat breakfast, and then gather my testing supplies, double-checking to make sure that I have not forgotten anything.

I calmly walk to the testing site from my hotel room. I soon arrive at the bar exam testing location. Although I have a sense of anticipation, I am not nervous or anxious. I stand in line, waiting to be admitted to the testing center. I see people reviewing their notes, but I do not need to do this. I have learned more than enough to pass the bar exam, and reviewing notes now is unnecessary.

The line begins to move. After a few minutes, I present my identification to the person at the door and enter the testing center. I put my backpack and snacks in the location designated. I remove my laptop and other supplies from my backpack. I check to make sure I have everything I need. Then, I walk toward the door to the testing area.

I walk into a large room, filled with row upon row of tables and chairs. The room is big and filled with noise as people set up their computers and exchange small talk. It takes a few moments, but I eventually locate my seat. I look around and note where the exits are in case I need to go to the bathroom during the test. I plug in my computer and turn it on. While my computer is booting up, I arrange my other testing supplies (watch, pens, etc.) on the table. Once my computer has started up, I open my testing software and sit calmly, awaiting instructions.

After everyone is seated, the exam proctor reviews the exam instructions. Even though the instructions seem mundane, I listen intently. I do not want to miss any important details about how to take the test.

The proctor tells us to begin. I open my package of essay questions, read the first one, and apply the techniques I have been practicing for so many weeks.

When people begin typing their answers, it sounds like a hard rainstorm, even through my earplugs. I am amazed at how loud it is. The noise does not bother me though because I have practiced writing essays in noisy environments. I work efficiently and calmly, analyzing and answering the questions asked of me.

(3) Writing a great essay

I am calm. I look at the essay question in the examination booklet. I first look to the questions at the end of the fact pattern so that I know what to look for when I read the fact pattern. Then, I slowly, methodically read the fact pattern. I do not rush. There is plenty of time to accomplish all of my tasks. If I rush this part of the essay-writing process, I may miss issues that will cost me valuable points.

As I read through the fact pattern, I prepare a list of issues that relate to the questions asked of me. I will use this list as the basis of my outline for my essay.

I next call to mind the applicable laws, tests, and elements and add them to my outline. Now that I have identified all the issues and applicable law, I go through the fact pattern again, much more quickly this time, looking for facts to fill in the details of my outline.

My outline complete, I am ready to begin writing. I start typing my essay into my computer. I have practiced writing essays so many times that I write with ease and confidence. I follow my outline, and the words flow.

When I finish my essay, I still have some time left, so I read through it to correct any typing mistakes and to see if there is anything I can explain better. I tell myself that I have written a great essay.

[Note: if your system for writing essays is different from the steps listed in this visualization, you should modify your visualization script to match your particular process.]

(4) Writing a great performance test

I take a deep breath to calm myself. When the proctor gives permission, I open the performance test booklet. I have practiced writing performance tests many times, and I follow my procedure during the examination.

I review the assignment memorandum in the file. Next I quickly review the library, looking for anything that might be useful for my answer.

Now, I review the entire file, noting facts that seem to relate to the assignment memorandum and information contained in the library.

Next, I read the assignment memorandum again very carefully and review the format guidelines memorandum, if there is one.

Now, I'm ready to write down the major topics in outline format. After I create this skeleton outline, I carefully review the library and fill in the various legal tests and statutory language that is relevant to the topics listed in my outline.

Next, I carefully read through the file to locate facts applicable to the legal authority that I have culled from the library and placed in my outline. I put these facts in my outline as well.

After quickly reviewing my outline to make sure that I have covered all the necessary information and that it is organized in a logical manner, I begin to write my answer based upon my outline.

I write quickly and efficiently but without haste. My performance test answer flows almost effortlessly now.

It was a lot of work, but I finish my answer with several minutes to spare. With the extra time, I review my answer and correct any spelling or grammatical mistakes. After reading through my answer, I know that I have written a very good, passing performance test.

[Note: if your system for writing performance tests is different from the steps listed in this visualization, you should modify your visualization script to match your particular process.]

(5) Doing well on the MBE

Today is the day when I take the multiple-choice portion of the bar exam. I am confident that I will do well. I have studied thoroughly all six subjects to be tested on the multiple-choice exam.

When I first began studying the multiple-choice questions, I was sometimes tricked by the way in which the questions were asked or the way in which the answers were phrased. Fortunately, I have practiced with enough questions and reviewed enough questions to understand how to approach this portion of the bar exam and how to score well on this portion of the bar exam.

I have three hours to answer 100 questions before the first break. After that, I will have three hours to answer 100 more questions. Three hours is more than enough time to analyze and answer 100 multiple-choice questions.

When the proctor tells me to begin the test, I open the booklet and begin reading the first question. I understand the question and review all of the suggested answers. I quickly narrow the responses down to the correct answer and fill in the bubble on my answer sheet.

I work efficiently through all of the questions, filling in the bubble for the correct answer for each question. I finish my first hundred questions with time to spare, and go back over the handful of questions about which I was unsure.

During the lunch break, I do not dwell on any questions from the morning session. I enjoy my lunch, and avoid negative talk about the exam with my fellow examinees.

The second half of the multiple-choice test goes much like the first half. I work my way through the questions efficiently and confidently. Again I finish with some time to spare and review the few questions about which I was unsure.

When the proctor states that time is up and the test is over, I turn in my testing materials with a smile on my face. I have done very well on the MBE.

(6) Receiving your passing results

Today is the day that bar exam results will be available on line. I am slightly nervous, but confident that I passed.

At the time the exam results become available, I go to my computer. I take a deep breath and open my Internet browser. I go to the results web page.

After entering any necessary identification or password, I see that my name appears on the pass list. I am so happy. I shout out loud with joy. I call or text my friends and family to let them know the good news.

I knew I could do it. This is just confirmation of all my hard work and determination over the past few months. Soon, after I am sworn in, I will be a lawyer.

(7) Attending the swearing-in ceremony.

Today is the culmination of everything that I have worked for and I become a lawyer. I am so happy and so proud. I knew I could do it. It took a lot of work and sacrifice, but it was worth it.

I arrive at the swearing in ceremony with my [*husband/wife; boyfriend/girlfriend; parents; friends*]. There are a lot of people here. I see some friends from law school. We congratulate each other.

I have to fill out some paperwork before the ceremony, so I wait in line to do so.

After I complete the paperwork, I find a place to sit in the auditorium. Several distinguished lawyers, judges, and justices are sitting at the podium table in front of the auditorium. Normally, I would dread sitting through their droning speeches, but today I look forward to what they will say to welcome me into the guild.

When the speeches are over, the judge leading the ceremony asks everyone to stand and be sworn in. I raise my right hand and repeat the words of the oath.

I am now a lawyer.

Conclusion

Please do not limit yourself to the topics and scripts discussed in this chapter. If you have a particular concern that keeps nagging at you, spend time visualizing how you will deal with it should it arise.

For example, in July 2008, an earthquake struck during the administration of the bar exam in California. While there was no damage or injury from the quake, I am sure certain people were rattled by it. As another example, when I took the bar exam in Oregon, the testing center had a problem providing enough power for all of the laptop users. Circuit breakers kept shutting off randomly throughout the testing area, and the start of the exam was delayed about 30 minutes. People were freaking out at the thought of having to handwrite the exam.

Visualizing unexpected moments and how you will recover from them is useful for remaining calm during the bar exam. Even if the situation you visualize never occurs, another unanticipated situation may occur, and having dealt with something similar in your visualization, you can adapt quickly to the situation that presents itself.

As you can see, positive visualization is a very useful tool for building confidence going into the bar exam. By repeatedly visualizing your successful completion of the bar exam, your Bar Exam Mind will want to make that successful completion a reality.

╬

CHAPTER THREE
AFFIRMATIONS

"I'm good enough. I'm smart enough. And doggone it, people like me."

– Stuart Smalley, *Saturday Night Live*

When many people think of affirmations, they have a stereotyped vision of something like the Stuart Smalley quote on the previous page. For those of you who don't know, Stuart Smalley was a character created by Al Franken on Saturday Night Live. Stuart hosted a late-night cable show in which he found the positive in all sorts of terrible or ridiculous situations.

While the Smalley sketches may have been funny, they did not reveal the true force behind affirmations. Affirmations are not a way of ignoring the difficult or troubling situations in which we find ourselves. Instead, they are useful to help us move beyond those situations.

What is an affirmation?

Affirmations are short, strong, and positive statements that train your mind to believe you can achieve your goals and aspirations. It is an affirmative statement that something has *already* come to pass. For example, if your goal is to lose weight, you might use the affirmation, "I am fit and attractive" or "I love having a healthy and fit body."

In many ways, affirmations are like a shortened visualization. To say an affirmation takes much less time than to perform a visualization, but can have much of the same power. In fact, some experts on visualization suggest that you say an affirmation before starting a visualization exercise and after completing it.

Affirmations may be recited silently, spoken aloud, or written down. The important thing with affirmations is repetition. By repeating a *positive* affirmation, we crowd out any *negative* thoughts from our mind that might be preventing us from achieving our goals.

The easiest way to incorporate affirmations into your life is to set aside five or ten minutes each day to repeat affirmations silently to yourself. Ideal times to do this are in the morning upon waking and at night before falling asleep. You might also try reciting affirmations while waiting at stop lights or standing in line at the market, bank, or anywhere else.

As I explain at the end of this chapter, it is fairly easy to create your own affirmations targeted for your goals and for overcoming doubts or other negative thoughts peculiar to your bar exam situation. In the meanwhile, here are some affirmations that are likely to be useful to you while preparing for the bar exam:

- ➤ I enjoy my life.
- ➤ My mind stores and recalls information with ease.
- ➤ Everything I do helps me fulfill my life's purpose.
- ➤ I am relaxed and calm.
- ➤ Each day, my life gets better and better.
- ➤ I now have a satisfying job as an attorney.
- ➤ The universe is abundant; there is plenty for all of us.
- ➤ I have plenty of time to do all the things I want to do.
- ➤ My brain is healthy and beautiful.
- ➤ I am healthy and beautiful.
- ➤ I deserve success and happiness.
- ➤ I study for the bar exam easily and effortlessly.

Commitment, Consistency, and Writing

Affirmations are a way to ensure that we commit to a goal and act consistently with that commitment. In chapter three of his wonderful book *Influence*, psychologist Robert Chaldini speaks of the power commitment and consistency. His purpose is to show his readers how to extract compliance from others and how to understand when others are trying to extract compliance from them. Understandably, Chaldini has become something of a guru for salespeople and marketers, but his book has lessons for people who are trying to achieve goals, such as passing the bar exam.

Chaldini's thesis with respect to commitment and consistency is that if you make a commitment or take a stand publicly and "on the record," it sets the stage for *automatic* consistency with that earlier commitment. Thus, a salesperson tries to get you to buy something really inexpensive, because once you buy something at any price, you are committed to being a customer. Once having made that commitment, it is much easier for the salesperson to sell you something more expensive because you have already purchased something from the salesperson.

Similarly, Chaldini recounts experiments demonstrating that homeowners who signed a petition in favor of state beautification are statistically much more likely to agree to display a "Drive Carefully" sign on their lawns than people who were not ever asked to sign the petition. Why? Those who signed the petition had committed themselves as public-spirited citizens who cared about public service.

Chaldini provides many other examples to arrive at the conclusion that our own behavior informs us about ourselves and influences our future actions. In fact, our own behavior is the *primary source* of information about our own beliefs, values and attitudes.

A central source of our understanding of our own identity is what we have written. According to Chaldini (and I agree), if we write something down, it is much harder to distance ourselves from the belief memorialized in that writing. In fact, if someone else saw the writing, they would almost certainly assume that we truly believed what we wrote, even if we were just doing a bizarre thought experiment or writing first-person fiction.

How does this apply to affirmations and the Bar Exam Mind?

A central feature of a Bar Exam Mind is to be confident and focused in your studies and calm in your attitude toward the test itself. While mentally rehearsing visualizations and affirmations to yourself is a central part of creating the Bar Exam Mind, writing down at least some visualizations and affirmations is important as well.

Chaldini's commitment and consistency theory can be applied to many of the ideas discussed in this book. You can write out your visualization scripts to make them more concrete. You can write out your affirmations repeatedly. You can also enter into a contract to pass the bar exam between your current self and your future lawyer self. (See Appendix D for a sample contract.)

Written exercise

A powerful technique for crowding negative thoughts and doubts from your mind is to write a series of affirmations repeatedly. For many people, especially people who have spent years in an educational system based on the written word, the physical act of writing helps solidify ideas more effectively than just speaking the idea.

Obviously, you can use this technique with any affirmations. Let me suggest, however, that you begin with the following exercise: Get a piece of paper. Then, write the following three-part affirmation at least ten times.

I passed the bar exam.

[Name], you passed the bar exam!

[Name] passed the bar exam.

By writing the affirmation in these various forms, you have written the affirmation in all of its possible permutations. That is, (1) you say it to yourself, (2) you hear people telling the affirmation to you, and (3) you hear people talking about you in the third-person with others.

After you write this three-part affirmation at least ten times, be sure you write affirmations about your career as a lawyer:

I am a successful lawyer.

[Name], you are a successful lawyer.

[Name] is a successful lawyer.

At first, this exercise might seem somewhat ridiculous, but it is really powerful. You should perform this written exercise once per week as you prepare for the bar exam.

To the extent that you experience doubt or resistance to the goal you are affirming in writing, pause briefly to write any such thoughts on a separate piece of paper and then continue writing your affirmations. Once you have finished the affirmations, you can return to the "resistance" statements, and contemplate them and see if they are true obstacles. If they are, consider how you can surmount those obstacles. Perhaps you should revisit the Stoic-inspired negative visualization exercise in Chapter One, and add these concerns to your various lists, if they have not already been addressed there.

Make your own affirmations

When you first start using affirmations, is easiest to use affirmations created by someone else. That is why I have provided affirmations for you earlier in this chapter. Nevertheless, affirmations are more powerful when you create them yourself.

It is quite easy to make your own affirmations. If you follow a few simple steps, you can make affirmations that will be very effective in helping you calm anxiety, reduce stress, and create the confidence to succeed on the bar exam. These affirmations will help you create your Bar Exam Mind.

First, you should phrase affirmations in the present tense. Instead of saying "I will be a lawyer when I pass the bar exam," you should say, "I am a lawyer." By doing this, you create the reality in your mind that will then manifest in physical reality.

Affirmations should be made in short, positive statements. Because it is the repetition of affirmations that makes them so powerful, if they are stated in a negative way, this will have a profoundly detrimental effect on you. If the affirmation is phrased positively, it will have a profoundly positive effect on you and the reality that you create in your life.

Finally, when you're reciting affirmations, you should put your mind in a state where you believe the affirmation is true. Effectiveness of affirmations is highly correlated to your *belief* that what you are affirming will come to pass. Effectiveness is less closely correlated to the *quantity* of affirmations you recite.

Conclusion

Affirmations are an extremely powerful adjunct to the practice of visualization. I have used both affirmations and visualizations to great success in my life. In particular, I used visualizations to find my first job as an attorney after moving to California. I was having a hard time getting interviews because the economy had started its downturn in 2008. I tried networking and sending out resumes to numerous law firms, but had no success.

In my desperate state, I began to visualize working for a law firm. Before I went to bed, I visualized this job, including getting dressed for work in the morning, driving to work, meeting with clients, performing research, etc. In addition, I said various affirmations like "I have a good job as a lawyer" and "I go to work every morning at a law firm."

After doing this for about three weeks, I received a call from someone I had met for lunch several months earlier. He told me that his firm was hiring and that he would like me to come in for an interview. In a short time, I had a job offer.

Skeptics will say that I got this job because of networking efforts I made several months earlier. But, it seems to me that my earnest desire to get a job and my use of visualizations and affirmations in furtherance of that desire was what tipped the balance in my favor.

Tip the bar exam balance in your favor.

CHAPTER FOUR
START YOUR JOURNAL

"Wherever we go, whatever we do, self is the sole subject we study and learn."

— Emerson, *Journals*

"Self-reflection is the school of wisdom."

— Baltasar Gracián, *The Art of Worldly Wisdom*

"No man can produce great things who is not thoroughly sincere in dealing with himself."

— James Russell Lowell, *Rousseau and the Sentimentalists*

You should keep a journal during your bar exam preparations. Why? Because engaging in honest self-reflection is necessary to face a stressful and anxious situation as important as the bar exam.

If all you do is study, study, study, without spending time to assess the progress of your studies and what all the studying makes you think and feel about yourself and your future, you will not understand what is really happening in your mind. A fundamental requirement for the creation of a Bar Exam Mind is to understand how your mind works. You need to make sure that no negative thoughts or emotions are building up inside of you that might sabotage your ability to study for or pass the bar exam.

Through the process of journaling, you will filter your feelings and thoughts about the bar exam through objects of contemplation, such as a topic, quote, or question. In response to each object of contemplation, you will write whatever pops into your head, and you will keep writing for a minimum period of time.

The idea is that journaling will cleanse your mind of whatever it is that you were thinking that day. If you had anxieties, they will be lessened; if you were over-confident, it will be tempered by a realistic assessment of your current level of preparation. After completing a journaling session, you will be able to see the progress of your test preparation more clearly.

I recommend that you get a paper journal or notebook to write in. These can be purchased from any number of stores for a variety of prices, from the super-cheap to the astonishingly expensive. If you prefer a minimalist approach, you can just get a stack of paper and staple it together. While it is possible to record your thoughts on a word processor, it is better to get away from the technology for a few minutes and put your thoughts directly onto paper. Handwriting seems to have a contemplative effect that pushing keys has yet to equal. In the end, however, do whatever you feel most comfortable with to ensure that you will actually write journal entries.

This book includes several exercises for guided journaling, as well as a grab-bag of quotes (see Appendix A) for you to look through and respond to during days on which you choose to free-write. The most important thing when journaling it to write until you have nothing more to say. This serves two purposes: (1) you will take your thoughts to their logical conclusion and understand what you are truly thinking and feeling at that moment, and (2) you release all stress and anxiety through your writing and will feel better when you are done. If you do not feel that you have time to write for an extended period of time, make sure that you budget a minimum of 15 minutes for each journal entry, as it often takes 5 minutes for your thoughts to gain enough momentum so the words start flowing effortlessly onto the page.

Journaling Exercises

Below are four journaling exercises. When you follow the schedule at the front of the book, you will be asked to do these exercises on particular days. For now, just read through them so your subconscious mind can start thinking about them.

Exercise One

Make a list of everything you are thankful for and everything at which you have been successful. The purpose of doing this is to make sure that you have a baseline to go back to in the midst of bar exam study, when you may be having doubts about your ability to succeed at the bar exam. By having a list of successes and objects of gratitude, you understand that your life is measured by more than just a single test. This helps to ratchet down the pressure and stress that we impose upon ourselves to accomplish particular goals. By reminding ourselves that we have achieved much in our lives and that we are thankful for much that we have been given and achieved, the stress of a particular situation is reduced and often completely vanishes.

So take the time to put together a comprehensive list. Give yourself at least 15 minutes to do this, but if you are still writing after 15 minutes, keep writing until you have completed your list. Furthermore, if a day or two goes by and you think of something else to add to the list, come back and add to the list. Then, on days when you're feeling stressed out by the bar exam or feeling sorry for yourself because you can't go out with your friends one evening or you can't seem to learn a particular legal concept, refer to this list and think of how great it will feel when you add "passed the bar exam" to it.

Exercise Two

Review the following quotes and write about what they mean to you in the context of bar exam preparation.

"Lack of time is actually lack of priorities." – Timothy Ferriss, *The 4-Hour Workweek: Escape 9-5, Live Anywhere, and Join the New Rich*

"[Diligence is] the necessity of giving sufficient attention to detail to avoid error and prevail against obstacles." – Atul Gawande, *Better: A Surgeon's Notes on Performance*

Exercise Three

Whether you practice law for 30 years or never practice at all, a law degree and a bar license are achievements of which you should be proud. Write about how you will feel once you pass the bar exam and become a lawyer. Write about what great things you plan to do after you become a lawyer.

Exercise Four

Which three essay subjects do you hope appear on the bar exam? What about those subjects makes you confident in your ability to answer essay questions about them?

Now, which three subjects do you hope do not appear during the bar exam? Why do you feel this way? What can you do to prepare if those subjects show up on the bar exam? Do you need to change your study methods for those topics? Should you practice with these subjects more? Give this some serious thought.

Quote Grab Bag

At certain points in the Bar Exam Mind schedule, you will be asked to write a journal entry after reviewing the "Quote Grab Bag," located in Appendix A, and follow instructions. If this is your first time reading this chapter, go to Appendix A and just read through the quotes so your subconscious can start formulating a response to them.

Similarly, if you decide not to follow the 21-day schedule for some reason, you can use the Quote Grab Bag for inspiration when you are having trouble writing a journal entry.

Conclusion

This chapter has been somewhat short because journaling is what you make of it. That is, if you don't take the time to keep a journal consistently and you don't set aside enough time for each journaling exercise, journaling will not be very effective.

I advise you to take journaling very seriously. The writing is a form of therapy that will assist you in cleansing yourself of anxieties and stressors. This is, of course, sorely needed during bar exam preparation.

╫

CHAPTER FIVE
NUTRITION FOR LEARNING AND FOCUS

"Let food be your medicine and medicine be your food."

– Hippocrates

Your development of a Bar Exam Mind will be much more successful if you ensure that your body and brain are getting the nutrition they need to perform at optimal levels. What follows is a synthesis of information about how to nourish your brain to improve its physical functioning. With a healthy brain, you can focus and learn much better.

This chapter looks at diet (what to eat and what *not* to eat) and at supplements that improve focus and memory, lessen anxiety, and help you sleep.

Diet

Diet is a powerful tool to enhance and promote brain function. If you eat the right things, your ability to focus and retain knowledge will be enhanced. If you eat the wrong things, you will promote brain degeneration and hamper your ability to focus or retain knowledge.

In the last few years, the study of how diet influences brain formation, function, and degeneration has taken off. In fact, PBS now has a series of specials featuring Dr. Daniel G. Amen in which Dr. Amen teaches you how to prevent Alzheimer's and other degenerative diseases from affecting your brain. Brain health is in the mainstream.

1. *What not to eat*

Rather than start with a list of foods that are good for you, this chapter begins with a list of foods are bad for you. Once you know what to avoid in order to maintain good brain functioning, it tends to be rather easy to exclude those foods if you make the effort to do so.

According to Dr. David Perlmutter, author of *The Better Brain Book*, the most important thing to avoid are trans-fats and saturated fats. He says that the worst fats of all are the trans-fatty acids, which, as you are probably aware, are found in fried foods, margarine, and most processed baked goods. According to Perlmutter, saturated fats found in animal products are also to be avoided. Dr. Perlmutter says that these fats promote inflammation in the brain and prevent good fats, like fish oil or olive oil, from getting into your brain cells. He says that trans-fatty acids and saturated fats can make your brain cells hard and rigid and interfere with your brain's ability to process information quickly. Obviously, a slow brain is something you want to avoid during the bar exam and for the rest of your life.

In what seems like a great paradox, both sugar *and* artificial sweeteners are bad for your brain. There is evidence that aspartame, normally sold under the brand name Equal, may be toxic to your brain. Aspartame contains chemicals called excitotoxins which, according to Dr. Perlmutter, can cross the brain/blood barrier and overstimulate brain cells, disrupting normal production of neurotransmitters and promoting free radicals. This can cause mood swings, headaches, and even promote the growth of brain tumors. In a situation as intense as bar exam preparation, one should avoid foods that could cause major headaches or mood swings.

The second half of the paradox is sugar problem. There are studies that show the people who eat sweets on a regular basis are at increased risk of elevated levels of blood sugar, which increases the risk of developing memory problems at an earlier age than normal. There's also evidence that eating sweets may lead to Parkinson's disease later in life. While the risks of excess sugar consumption may not have a direct impact on a young person studying for the bar exam, if you can use the bar exam as a motivation to break your sugar habit now, you will have a better brain in the future and be able to practice law well into later life.

You should also be cautious about your consumption of alcohol. Most medical professionals agree that one to two servings of alcoholic beverages each day reduces the risk of neurological disease, but consumption of more than two servings of alcohol per day increases the risk. The mechanism by which alcohol increases this risk is that as the liver purifies alcohol from the body, it depletes glutathione, which is the brain's primary antioxidant.

So, if you are a drinker, it is okay to keep drinking while studying for the bar exam, but do so in moderation. In addition to a reduced risk of neurological disease in the long-term, the moderate consumption of alcohol, in a short-term may help reduce some of the stress of studying for the bar exam.

Finally, it should go without saying that you should avoid illegal drugs at any time, but especially while studying for the bar exam. Neither the short- nor long-term effects of illegal drugs on the brain have been well studied, so why make yourself a guinea pig?

2.   *What to eat*

The basic recipe for a healthy, high-functioning brain is simple: eat more good fat, add antioxidants your diet, and get poisons off your plate. You need good fats because your brain is made of fat and needs more fat than any other nutrient. If you eat unhealthy fats, your brain will be unhealthy. Like all parts of your body, your brain is vulnerable to free radical attack, so you need to eat lots of antioxidant rich foods, mainly colorful vegetables and fruits. Unfortunately, many fruits and vegetables are treated with powerful pesticides that can cause significant damage to your brain and nervous system. Therefore, you need to eat the cleanest, healthiest food possible.

a.   Good fat

The two most brain-friendly fats are monounsaturated fat and polyunsaturated fat. Monounsaturated fats are the best fats for brain function, and are found in olive oil, canola oil[3], nuts and avocados. Because monounsaturated fats are high in antioxidants, they're less prone to damage from free radicals after they are incorporated into your brain cells.

Polyunsaturated fats include essential fatty acids: omega-3 and omega-6. Omega-3 fatty acids are important for the production of DHA which is important for effective cognitive function, and helps to avoid depression, moodiness, irritability, and slow reaction time. (For more on DHA, see the discussion of fish oil in the section on supplements below.) Omega-3 fatty acids are found in many kinds of fish, dark green vegetables, flax seeds, and pumpkin seeds. Omega-6 fatty acids, on the other hand, promote inflammation and free radical production, and therefore are not good for your brain. Most people get far too much omega-6 fatty acids in their diet because they are found in

---

[3] There is mounting evidence that canola oil and other cooking oils that have come into use during the last 100 years break down rapidly under exposure to sunlight and heat, and transform into trans-fats before we eat them. Therefore, to be most safe, stick with cooking oils that do not break down when heated, such as olive oil and coconut oil. For more on this issue, see *Deep Nutrition* by Dr. Cate Shanahan.

corn oil, peanut oil, and sunflower oil, which are common ingredients in most processed food.

b.   Antioxidants

Antioxidants are necessary to prevent free radicals from damaging your brain. A free radical is any atom or molecule that has a single unpaired electron in an outer shell. This means that free radicals are highly reactive and cause oxidative damage to your cells. The accumulated free radical damage leads to aging of cells and organs and related loss of function. Thus, antioxidants prevent the oxidative damage and slow the aging process.

The best way to get antioxidants into your diet is to eat at least six servings of vegetables and two servings of fruit every day. A serving is half a cup of cooked vegetables, 1 cup of raw vegetables, or one medium-sized fruit. Most of the antioxidants in fruits and vegetables are in the pigments of the plants. Therefore, different colored fruits and vegetables have different types of antioxidants. Generally, the more intense the color of the plant, the more antioxidants it has. So, you should eat a variety of fruits and vegetables throughout the day.

The simplest way to do this is to eat a mixed green salad every day. It is better to do this when lettuces are in season, typically during the cooler months of the year, because vegetables have more nutrients when they are grown during the correct season. In addition to lettuces, eat leafy greens and related vegetables. These are known as cruciferous vegetables and include plants like broccoli, watercress, mustard greens, kale, collard greens, chard, cauliflower, and broccoli.

If eating six servings of fruits and vegetables a day doesn't seem possible, you can always use supplements. Among the most powerful antioxident supplements are açaí berry and pomegranate. They can be purchased in a juice form or pill form depending on which is most convenient for you.

c.   Eat clean food

The easiest way to eat clean food is to buy organic produce, naturally-raised meat (e.g., grass-fed beef), and wild caught fish. Many studies show that organically grown produce contains significantly more vitamins and minerals than produce not grown organically. If you can't find organic produce or if it is simply too expensive, make sure you thoroughly wash your fruits and vegetables with a mild soap solution and peel fruits and vegetables that may be covered with a waxy coating.

d.   Drink a lot of water

Most people have heard that their body is 70% water, but did you know your brain is 80% water? It should be plainly obvious from these statistics that you should drink lots of water to maintain normal health, but especially so when you are placing your brain and body under stress, which you are doing while you study for the bar exam.

According to Dr. Amen, even slight dehydration increases the body's stress hormones. Since part of having a Bar Exam Mind is to learn ways to reduce stress during your bar studies and during the bar exam itself, anything you can do to prevent an increase in stress hormones is important.

How much water should you drink? Many authorities state that you should take your weight and divide it in half to equal the number of ounces per day of water you should drink. Therefore, if you weigh 180 pounds, you should drink 90 ounces (2.7 liters) of water per day.

Supplements

Obviously, the best thing you can do for brain health is to eat well. But let's face it, most of us cannot eat the perfect food all the time. So, while you should do your best to eat well during bar exam preparation, you may need to supplement your diet with vitamins, minerals, amino acids, and herbs.

The following section contains a list of supplements that will help your focus and memory, help alleviate anxiety, and assist you in getting a good night's sleep, all of which are important to effective bar exam study.

The basis for this list comes from four books: *Change Your Brain, Change Your Body* by Dr. Daniel G. Amen; *The Better Brain Book* by Dr. David Perlmutter; *The Mood Cure*, by Julia Ross; and *Mind Boosters*, by Dr. Ray Sahelian. Even though the supplements are recommended by trained medical professionals, before you begin using any of the supplements, you should check with your own health care provider to make sure these supplements will not have side effects on you or interfere with any medications you may be currently taking.

1. *Supplements for focus and memory*

- Acetyl-l-carnitine (ALC)
- B vitamins
- Coenzyme Q-10
- Fish oil (DHA)
- Ginko Biloba
- Zinc
- Choline
- DMAE
- Sage

Acetyl-l-carnitine (ALC) increases energy in the brain which helps enhance memory and concentration. ALC works by allowing essential nutrients to get into mitochondria to create energy. In addition to its central role in cellular energy production, ALC helps remove toxins from mitochondria to keep them functioning at optimal levels. Studies have shown that long-term use of ALC slows the progress of Alzheimer's Disease. Recommended dosage for adults is 500 mg twice a day. Within an hour or two of taking ALC, a typical response is to feel increased arousal and vigilance as well as mood improvement. These effects can last all day.

B vitamins. This complex of vitamins is important to the functioning of the nervous system and neurotransmitters in the brain that affect mood and thinking. Therefore it is important to ensure that you have proper intake of B vitamins in stressful and anxiety-inducing situations, such as preparation for the bar exam. Vitamin B6 is necessary for proper nervous system and brain function. Low levels of vitamin B-12 can result in confusion and depression. B12 is also needed to help control inflammation in the brain. Therefore is recommended that you take a B complex vitamin each day containing at least 50 mg of B6 and 500 mcg of B12. Be careful about taking a big dose of B vitamins in the afternoon or evening as it can cause agitation and interfere with sleep.

Coenzyme Q-10 is critical for brain health, and Dr. Perlmutter recommends that everyone takes it. There is a growing consensus among the scientific community that loss of Q-10 in the body as we age causes a decline in mental function. Coenzyme Q-10 is involved in the production of energy in the mitochondria, and because the brain is one of the most energy-intensive organs in the body it needs a large supply of Q-10 to perform its vital tasks. Q-10 is found mainly in fish and meat, so many doctors believe it is important for vegetarians and vegans to supplement their diets with it. Recommended daily dose for healthy people is 30 mg per day. Higher doses of Q-10 are available, but not recommended as they can induce restlessness and insomnia. (People taking blood thinners should not take Q-10 without first consulting their doctors.)

Fish oil, especially oil containing DHA (docosahexaenoic acid), is essential for the maintenance of normal brain function throughout life. Approximately 25% of the human brain is composed of DHA, and without enough DHA in your brain, you may become depressed and you may not be as alert or focused as you can be. If there is not enough DHA available in your body for the brain to use to repair itself and make new brain cells, your brain will start using saturated fat and trans-fatty acids do the job, making your brain cells hard and rigid. Fish oil has also been shown to calm down overactive brain signals, potentially increasing the ability to focus, and has been shown to stabilize nerve cells.

A typical fish oil dosage for adults is 1 to 2 g per day, but some doctors recommend up to 4 g per day. If you decide to take a DHA-only supplement rather than fish oil, a recommended daily dose is 300 mg per day.

I am a huge believer in the power of fish oil and take at least 2 g per day (which is about 1.5 teaspoons of my favorite brand, Liquid Nordic Naturals). When I am taking fish oil, I feel more focused, smarter, and more emotionally stable. These are helpful qualities to have when studying for the bar exam.

Ginkgo Biloba is a powerful antioxidant known to enhance circulation, memory, and concentration. Ginkgo is a good supplement to take if you suffer from low energy or decreased concentration. However, you should know there is a small risk of bleeding in the body, so be sure to consult with your doctor before you take ginkgo, especially if you're using blood thinning medication. A typical adult dose is 60 to 120 mg twice per day.

Zinc is a mineral that is found in foods such as red meat, poultry, legumes, nuts, and whole grains. Studies have linked zinc deficiency to mental lethargy. A typical adult dose is 25 to 80 mg per day, and should not exceed 100 mg. Zinc should be taken with food or juice to avoid nausea.

Choline is necessary for the creation of the neurotransmitter acetylcholine which is necessary for normal brain function. Choline is especially useful long-term because it may prevent Alzheimer's disease and dementia, but short-term it can help contribute to normal brain function. You can get choline from egg yolks, liver, peanuts, fish, milk, and cauliflower. If you don't eat these foods on a regular basis, the recommended dosage per day is 300 to 1200 mg. Choline pills can give you a boost in focus, which could be useful on days that you are having trouble concentrating. A dose of 250 to 500 mg taken in the morning can increase focus for the entire day. Note that a high intake of choline is associated with increased body warmth and possible gastrointestinal issues.

DMAE, like choline, is a precursor to the neurotransmitter of acetylcholine. It is used to increase the capacity of neurons in the brain and to increase attention span and memory abilities. (As an added bonus, DMAE appears to decrease wrinkles and improve lip shape, fullness, and the overall appearance of skin.) Typical recommended adult dosage is 300 to 500 mg per day.

Sage has long been believed to improve memory, and recent scientific evidence has confirmed that hypothesis. For improved mood and alertness, a typical dose is 300 to 600 mg per day of dried sage leaf capsules or 25 to 50 microliters of essential oil.

2.   *Supplements for anxiety and sleep*

- Ashwagandha
- Kava Kava
- 5-HTP
- Valerian
- Melatonin

Ashwagandha is a shrub found in India, Nepal, and Pakistan. It has properties that help the body better handle stress, anxiety, and fatigue. Its use can enable one to focus better because the focus-destroyers of stress, anxiety, and fatigue are treated by use of this plant. (Be careful, this herb is revered as an aphrodisiac as well!) Because ashwagandha can cause drowsiness in some people, it is recommended you take it in the evening after your day's work is over. A typical dose of Ashwagandha is about 500 mg in capsule form.

Kava Kava comes from a root of a South Pacific Peppertree. It is recommended by some doctors to promote sleep, reduce anxiety, and reduce the physical and emotional side effects of stress. Dr. Amen says that it works quickly as best suited for short-term sleeping problems, such as to promote sleep the night before a big test or presentation. Dr. Amen warns that you should not take the supplement every day because it may harm the liver. Furthermore, kava kava will adversely interact with alcohol, barbiturates, certain antidepressants, and numerous other drugs. You should not take kava kava, if you are pregnant or breast-feeding or before you drive a car. The typical adult dose is 150 to 300 mg one to three times per day as needed, or before bedtime.

5-HTP is an amino acid that is a building block for serotonin. Use of this supplement will increase serotonin, which may help control stress and improve sleep. In fact, some doctors prescribe this as a sleep aid, especially for those patients who have trouble "turning off" their brains at night or who have anxious thoughts that keep them awake. 5-HTP can cause upset stomach so one should start by taking small doses. Because 5-HTP is known to boost serotonin levels, some medical professionals use it to treat depression, but note that 5-HTP should not be taken with other medicines that increase serotonin, such as most antidepressant medications, unless you're closely supervised by your doctor. A typical dose to aid with sleep is 25 to 50 mg on an empty stomach about one hour before bed. Because 5-HTP can induce drowsiness it should not be taken during the day or when planning to operate heavy machinery.

I can speak from experience as to the effects of 5-HTP. I typically take a 50 mg dose of 5-HTP right before bedtime. It seems to help me sleep through the night, as I had great difficulty doing this for many years. Since taking 5-HTP regularly, I am able to sleep through the night almost every time. I have not had any problems with upset stomach, but I rarely take more than 50 mg at a time.

Valerian is an herb typically used as a sleep aid and an anti-stress medication. For thousands of years, people have used valerian as a treatment for insomnia as well as nervousness, stress, and pain. It can take up to two or three weeks to start feeling the effects of valerian, so it is not a good short-term sleep aid. Never take valerian with alcohol, barbiturates or other tranquilizers, and it should not be used during pregnancy or when breast-feeding. A typical adult dosage is 150 to 450 mg as capsule or infusion.

Melatonin is a hormone made in the brain that helps regulate the body's sleep cycle. Darkness stimulates the production of melatonin while light decreases the production of melatonin. Certain studies have shown that melatonin is effective in decreasing the time required to fall asleep, increasing the number of hours one stays asleep, and improving one's alertness. Melatonin is recommended to help alleviate symptoms of jet lag. Melatonin is generally considered safe and non-addictive. A typical dose to help with sleep is 0.3 to 1 mg taken on an empty stomach 30 to 90 minutes before bed. Melatonin is available in time-release capsules that can help maintain consistent sleep throughout the night. Tolerance to melatonin can build up quickly, so it is best to only take it periodically and only for a few consecutive nights. (See Appendix E for a discussion of my experiment with melatonin.)

Lifestyle Choices

Beyond what you eat and drink, your other personal habits can have a tremendous effect on the health of your brain. The following is a brief discussion of certain personal habits that have a negative effect on the ability of your brain to function at peak levels.

1. *Lack of sleep*

Probably the number one bad habit that people have is failure to get seven to eight hours of sleep per night. Studies have shown that missing a single night of sleep has an immediate effect on your brain function. Tests of mental ability repeatedly show that people who are sleep-deprived score lower than those who are well-rested.

Lack of sleep can also lead to increased stress hormones circulating in the body. If you are having trouble sleeping during your bar exam preparations, consider using some of the supplements discussed above.

2. *Failure to exercise*

Another bad habit is the failure to exercise on a regular basis. I was guilty of this while studying for the Oregon bar exam. As the weeks of studying passed, my back began to hurt more and more. At the time, I attributed this increased pain to the numerous hours of sitting. This was only half correct.

As a practicing lawyer, I now spend most of the day sitting, but my back problems have not reappeared because I exercise regularly. When your entire body is strong, it can take extended sedentary periods.

As for the brain, physical activity will increase blood flow to the brain which makes you feel more alert. This is why, if you feel yourself about to nod off while studying, you should get up, go outside, and walk around for a few minutes. In short, be sure to include regular exercise in your life during bar exam preparation.

3.   *Limit caffeine and alcohol*

I know this might be tough for some readers. When it comes to the brain, the main reason to limit these two substances is because they cause dehydration. The brain is 80% water, so dehydration of the brain will decrease its ability to function.

It should also be noted that not all caffeinated beverages are created equal. Numerous studies have shown that people who drink 2 to 3 cups of green tea per day have DNA that looks younger than people who do not drink 2 to 3 cups of green tea per day.

Conclusion

It is clear that proper nutrition, judicious supplementation, and certain lifestyle choices have a strong effect on the functioning of your brain and its ability to handle stress and anxiety. This chapter has provided you with various ways to improve your brain and your ability to study for and perform well on the bar exam.

Whether to implement any of the information in this chapter is up to you in consultation with a health care professional. Any time you make changes in your diet, exercise, or other routines, it can be difficult. So, pick and choose carefully any changes you will make. The last thing you should do when studying for the bar exam is adopt a change that will increase your stress or anxiety.

╬

CHAPTER SIX
ANTICIPATION OF CONDITIONS

"One unable to dance blames the unevenness of the floor."

– Malay Proverb

The concept of "anticipation of conditions" as it relates to bar exam preparation requires, to the greatest extent possible, you study and practice for the bar exam under conditions as similar as possible to the real bar examination. This is important for reasons similar to why positive visualization is important. As discussed in Chapter Two, the purpose of positive visualization is to assist your mind to create a reality you want, in this case, passing the bar exam.

The anticipation of conditions helps your mind and your body prepare for what you will face when actually taking the test. You will learn how to focus for the right number of hours, you will practice segments of the test under timed conditions in an environment similar to the bar exam, and you will get used to the rhythms of the bar exam so that when the real test is upon you, its intensity will not surprise and overwhelm you.

This chapter first discusses when and how much you should study, suggesting that you stick to a fairly rigid but temporally circumscribed schedule. The chapter next examines how and why to take practice tests, whether full-blown, day-long affairs, or short mini tests. Finally, this chapter discusses how to prepare for the experience of taking the bar exam at the examination site.

When and How to Study

Everyone has different ideas about how to study. For the bar exam, you need to have a predetermined schedule to stay on track and ensure you do not leave anything out. I believe the best approach is to choose a study schedule and stick with it until modification seems useful or necessary. The stability of the study schedule is also important so that you can focus on learning during the same time each day, and then on developing your Bar Exam Mind during the time you are not committed to studying black letter law.

Most bar preparation courses provide you with a study plan. The most well-known is BarBri's catchily-named "PACE Program." When I took BarBri for the Oregon exam, I tried to follow the PACE program for about . . . one day. It was clear to me that I would never have time to do all the work suggested by the PACE schedule. I had a wife and two children, and I was not going to abandon them for 70 hours a week so that I could keep up with a one-size-fits-all study program developed by someone who never met me and did not know my strengths and weaknesses.

Still, if you think the PACE Program will work for you, then follow it. I think it is unrealistic. Nevertheless, the decision to not follow the program can induce great anxiety in some people. Relax. Ask around; I bet very few of your friends and colleagues are keeping up with the PACE program either. The important thing is to put your mind at ease on this issue: *You can pass the bar exam without using the PACE program.* I did – twice.

If you decide to stick with the PACE program or whatever study schedule your bar prep course has given to you, great! You can ignore the rest of this section and move on to the "Taking Practice Tests" section on the next page.

If you have decided that the pre-formatted study schedule is not for you, what do you do instead? Design a study schedule for yourself. In order to design your own study program, you will need to determine the information you must learn, the amount of time you have to learn it, your strengths and weaknesses (e.g., are you a good writer but a bad multiple-choice test taker?) and your tolerance for sitting all by yourself reading black letter law, doing sample MBE questions, and writing out numerous essays and performance tests.

Once you make these determinations, you should review the number of subject areas you are required to master for the bar exam in your state. Then, determine how many days per week you will study in the time leading up to the bar exam. Lastly, schedule what you will study and when, and then stick to the schedule. Basically, you are creating a PACE-style study schedule that conforms to your own mental and life rhythms, which makes the schedule easier to follow.

If you want more detailed information on how to create your own study plan, see Appendix C in which I discuss how I prepared my own study plan for the California bar exam.

Taking Practice Tests

Once you have decided on your study schedule, you need to make sure it includes time for practice tests. The purpose of taking practice tests is two-fold: (1) to develop the endurance necessary to stay focused and perform at a high level during the hours- and days-long bar exam and (2) to learn to perform under actual exam conditions, which are usually far from ideal.

There are two kinds of practice tests. The first kind is a full-blown mock test, such as doing 200 mixed MBE questions in one day under timed conditions, just like you will do during the real bar exam. The purpose of doing a full-blown practice test is to ensure that you are able to focus for a complete testing day. This is a difficult task. Since you have recently graduated from law school, your ability to focus should be strong, but taking the bar exam is like having four final exams on each day for two or three straight days. It is qualitatively different than a law school examination.

The second kind of practice test is a mini test about a single subject or sub-area of a subject. These mini tests are important to do throughout your bar exam preparations because testing helps you solidify your knowledge of a given topic. Mini testing can be as simple as going through flash cards or doing 10 MBE questions, or as complex as trying to write an entire subject outline from memory.

1.   *Full-blown practice tests.*

If you are enrolled with BarBri, the company has a built-in practice bar exam where you show up at the class site and take a test in the same format and under the same time constraints as if you were taking your jurisdiction's real bar exam. This is a great tool and, if you take the test seriously, it will likely be sufficient preparation under this prong of my suggestions to you.

Now, by "take the practice test seriously," I mean that you should show up, give your best effort for the full time allowed, and get used to the *intensity* of the bar exam. Unless you are brilliant, your performance on the practice test will likely be far from a passing effort. But that does not matter because the point here is just to see how your body and mind react to being forced to test for several days in a row.

For those of you not taking BarBri or another review course that includes a sample bar examination, you need to build such practice into your study schedule. When I took the Oregon bar, I was taking BarBri and so used its practice test. When I studied for the California bar exam, I was doing it on my own and so had to build it in. I chose a Tuesday and a Wednesday about three weeks before the bar exam as practice exam days. Even though the California bar exam is a three-day exam, I only did a two-day practice exam. I did this for two reasons: 1) I had taken a bar exam before and was confident that if I could perform for two days, I could perform for three and 2) day three of the California bar has a format identical to day one, so I felt that studying rather than doing an identical practice test would be a better use of that extra day.

Another important thing to note is that I made the practice exam Tuesday and Wednesday. In most states, the bar exam starts on a Tuesday, and California is no exception. Furthermore, in states that use the MBE, it is *always* administered on a Wednesday. Therefore, to anticipate the conditions properly, I practiced the written portion (essays and performance tests) on Tuesday and practiced the multiple choice MBE portion on Wednesday. Had I chosen to do a three-day practice exam, I would have done the second written portion on Thursday. It is important to match the day of the week with the correct exam format so that your mind and body synchronize their abilities with the correct days of the week.

Finally, find out the approximate start time of your state's bar exam. Be sure that you start and stop your practice examination within those time parameters so that the practice session is as realistic as possible.

2. Mini tests

A "mini test" is a brief test of your knowledge on a single subject or subtopic. Examples of mini tests include: reviewing flashcards containing the elements of intentional torts, outlining a response to an essay question, writing down everything you can remember about subject matter jurisdiction, doing 20 criminal law MBE questions, or writing a full-length answer to a single essay question.

If you think that doing a single full-blown practice test is enough to prepare for the bar exam, then you need to change your thinking. By testing knowledge in small pieces, you actually solidify what you are learning much better than simply trying to memorize. Scientific studies have proven this.

A study published in the journal *Science* in January 2011 provides strong empirical evidence that practice tests matter, and not just full-blown practice tests. The main conclusion of the study was that "retrieval practice" testing helped students learn more about a topic than any other method.

Retrieval practice is quite simple: you study whatever you need to learn, then you take some time immediately after study to try and recall everything you just studied, then you compare what you remembered with what you studied to see what you missed, then you do another retrieval practice test. The second retrieval test solidifies the information in your mind.

It is clear that this format works well with small bits of information, but how to apply it to the bar exam monster?

One suggestion is to read your outline (or Conviser Mini Review, or whatever study source you have) on a particular topic, say Civil Procedure. Then do the retrieval practice as discussed above. This could be a bit cumbersome, trying to retrieve an entire outline all at once, so maybe a better approach would be to break an outline into chunks. Continuing with the Civil Procedure example, you might read the part of your outline that deals with subject matter jurisdiction, then try to retrieve it from memory, review your response and compare it with your outline, then try retrieving again. Then, move on to the next sub-topic.

Whether you use retrieval practice testing in addition to other forms of mini tests is up to you. The important take away from the *Science* study is that practice testing is a highly useful way to learn. You *must* include mini tests in your bar exam preparation. Success on mini tests will help build your Bar Exam Mind because it gives you added confidence and serenity going into the bar exam itself.

Practicing for Testing at the Testing Center

In addition to practicing for the endurance aspect of the bar exam, you need to practice for the auditory and visual experience of the bar exam. What I mean is that you need to be ready to take a test in a room with hundreds or even thousands of people, many of whom are panic-stricken and hyper-stressed. Because you will have cultivated your Bar Exam Mind, stress should not be much of a factor for you. However, if you neglect sensitizing yourself to the bar exam testing environment, you could have unsuspected repercussions when you are sitting for the actual exam.

Let me briefly describe my two bar exam experiences:

For the Oregon bar, there is only one testing location for the entire state. When I took the exam in July 2006, all 700 people taking the bar converged on a rented convention hall at a hotel by the Portland International Airport. The majority of these people were taking the test on a computer and were placed in the same room.

When I took the test, the room for those using computers had probably 500 people in it. All of these people had plugged their laptops into a series of daisy-chained extension cords and power strips. Shortly before the test was set to start, the power went out to a large portion of the room because the drain on the daisy-chained extension cords was too great. When the power went out, panic spread. Finally, the power was restored and the test started about 30-45 minutes late.

Once everyone started typing, it sounded like heavy rain. Thank goodness I had my earplugs in. The entire time I was typing I kept wondering if the power would go out. I kept checking my power cord to ensure the green "it's still working" light was glowing. What a distraction! Day two was better since we only needed pencils to take the MBE. There was still panic in the air and I noticed that several people actually did not bother to show up for the second day of the test, on the assumption that they had already failed.

In California, the number of people taking the exam as well as the size of the state requires that the bar examiners have several locations to administer the bar. I took the test in February 2008 in San Diego, where it seemed like there was a mere 800 or so people in a convention hall taking the test on their computers. I have heard that some locations of the

California bar exam have nearly 2,000 people taking the test in the same room.

With the California bar, the examiners seemed a lot more strict than those in Oregon. We had to put all of our test supplies in a clear plastic bag and leave our backpacks outside of the room. We had to provide fingerprints, signature cards, and photo ID during various moments of the exam. Ridiculous, silly, and distracting. At least I did not have to sit through the earthquake that hit during the July 2008 examination!

As you can see, any manner of things – anticipated and not anticipated – can occur during the bar exam. Therefore, you should conduct at least some of your practice testing under less-than-ideal conditions, so you can adapt to the expected and unexpected distractions and stressors that *may occur* during the actual bar exam.

Your first set of practice tests should be under ideal conditions: no distractions, limited noise. Once you have practiced all portions of the bar exam under ideal conditions, then introduce less-than-ideal conditions so that you can train yourself to perform at a high level even where there is noise and visual and other distractions.

I suggest that you set aside at least one block of time to practice essays (and, if your bar requires it, performance test writing) and another block of time to practice MBE questions (unless you are in one of those states that doesn't use the MBE; in that case, double your essay/PT prep). Once you have practiced at least one time under ideal conditions, locate a place where there will be a sizeable number of people who will be making at least some noise but where you will not likely be interrupted by someone speaking to you. Ideal places include a busy public library or a coffee shop.

Then, go to your chosen place and write an essay or a performance test under timed conditions and then do 33 MBE questions in one hour. Try to do this on two or three separate occasions. Of course, be sure to do it at the time of day when you would actually be doing the same thing for the bar examination.

Lastly, if your bar has odd rules for its exam, be sure to incorporate them into your anticipation of conditions practice. For example, the Virginia Bar requires that applicants take the bar examination wearing business attire. How would you like to fail because you weren't comfortable taking a test in a coat and tie (men) or wearing a tailored skirt or suit (women)? Therefore, be sure to do at least some of your practice testing incorporating any peculiar requirements of your state's bar examiners. Do not let yourself fail for a foolish reason and for lack of practice.

In summary, make sure you do a complete test under timed conditions and practice bite-sized portions of the bar exam under both favorable and unfavorable conditions.

Conclusion

A Bar Exam Mind is one that has trained for the rigors it will encounter during the bar examination itself. The mental preparation encouraged through visualizations and affirmations is necessary, but will not be as effective unless done in conjunction with endurance training for your mind, brain and body. Practice testing and simulation of adverse conditions is the endurance training you need.

╬

CONCLUSION

The creation of a Bar Exam Mind is a holistic endeavor. It requires the mental and emotional work of negative and positive visualizations, the positive reinforcement of affirmations, the cathartic and self-exploratory work of journaling, the care for the physical brain and body inherent in nutrition and lifestyle, and the endurance and rehearsal training of actually practicing for the examination. This book has shown you how to do all of these things.

One is not born with a Bar Exam Mind, but one can create a Bar Exam Mind. Now that you are at the end of this book, I hope that you agree with this statement. With your newly acquired skills, you will be able to study for the bar exam in a diligent and focused way, without anxieties and fears distracting you from your studies.

Good luck on the bar exam!

Please be sure to visit
www.barexammind.com
for additional information and techniques.

APPENDICES

APPENDIX A – QUOTE GRAB BAG

Instructions: Select a quote from the list below, contemplate the quote for at least five minutes, considering what it means for your bar exam preparations as well as for your overall life. Then, write a response to the quote in your journal.

◇ ◇ ◇

"To learn is a natural pleasure, not confined to philosophers, but common to all men." – Aristotle, *Poetics*

✦

"One should always think of what one is about; when one is learning, one should not think of play; and when one is at play, one should not think of one's learning." – Lord Chesterfield, *Letters to His Son*, July 24, 1739

✦

"Let a man accept his destiny, no pity and no tears." – Euripides, *Iphigenia in Tauris*

✦

"It usually takes a hundred years to make a law, and then, after it has done its work, it usually takes a hundred years to get rid of it." – Henry Ward Beecher, *Proverbs from Plymouth Pulpit*

✦

"The success of most things depends upon knowing how long it will take to succeed." – Montesquieu, *Pensées diverses*

✦

"Engineers conduct water, fletchers make arrows true, carpenters straighten wood, the well disciplined train themselves." – Buddha, "Violence", *The Dhammapadda*, tr. Thomas Cleary

✦

"Everyone must row with the oars he has." – English Proverb

✦

"A man's behavior is the index of the man, and his discourse is the index of his understanding." – Ali ibn-abi-Talib, *Sentences*

✦

"He who desires but acts not, breeds pestilence." – William Blake, "Proverbs of Hell," *The Marriage of Heaven and Hell*

✦

"Shallow men believe in luck . . . . Strong men believe in cause and effect." – Emerson, *The Conduct of Life*

✦

"Nowhere can man find a quieter or more untroubled retreat than in his own soul." – Marcus Aurelius, *Meditations*

✦

"There are times when fear is good. It must keep its watchful place at the heart's controls. There is advantage in the wisdom won from pain." – Aeschylus, *The Eumenides*

✦

"Do not consider painful what is good for you." – Euripides, *Medea*

✦

"Wherever law ends, tyranny begins." – John Locke, *Two Treatises on Government*

✦

"Lawyers and painters can soon change white to black." – Danish Proverb

✦

"If there were no bad people there would be no good lawyers." – Charles Dickens, *The Old Curiosity Shop*

✦

"Most [people] that do thrive in the world do forget to take pleasure during the time that they are getting their estate, but reserve that till they have got one, and then it is too late for them to enjoy it." – Samuel Pepys, *Diary*

✦

"Nothing is so uncertain or unpredictable as the feelings of a crowd." – Livy, *Ab Urbe Condita*

✦

"We are not machines that can produce the same output every day, endlessly." – Shakti Gawain, *The Path of Transformation*

✦

"The mightiest rivers lose their force when split up into several streams." – Ovid, *Love's Cure*

✦

"Divide the fire, and you will the sooner put it out." – Publilius Syrus, *Moral Sayings*

✦

"The law is the witness and external deposit of our moral life. Its history is the history of the moral development of the race." – Oliver Wendell Holmes, Jr.

✦

"Some circumstantial evidence is very strong, as when you find a trout in the milk." – Thoreau, *Journal*

✦

"Courage is a kind of salvation." – Plato, *The Republic*

✦

"For those who have completed their journey, left sorrow behind are free in all circumstances, and liberated from all bondage, affliction does not exist." – Buddha, "The Worthy", *The Dhammapadda*, tr. Thomas Cleary

✦

"There is no success without hardship." – Sophocles, *Electra*

✦

"Don't let life discourage you; everyone who got where he is had to begin where he was." – Richard L. Evans, *Time*, July 26, 1963

✦

"The reward of a thing well done is to have done it." – Emerson, "New England Reformers," *Essays: Second Series*

✦

"Education is an ornament in prosperity and a refuge in adversity." – Aristotle, as quoted in Diogenes Laertius' *Lives and Opinions of Eminent Philosophers*

✦

"He that can't endure the bad, will not live to see the good." – *Yiddish Proverbs*, ed. Hanan J. Ayalti

✦

"A just cause is not ruined by a few mistakes." – Dostoevsky

✦

"To win without risk is to triumph without glory." – Corneille, *The Cid*

✦

"Calmness is always Godlike." – Emerson, *Journals*

✦

"Laws and institutions must go hand in hand with the progress of the human mind." – Thomas Jefferson

✦

"Few things are impossible to diligence and skill." – Thomas Fuller, M.D., *Gnomologia*

✦

"We do not get good laws to restrain bad people. We get good people to restrain bad laws." – G. K. Chesterton, "Thoughts Around Koepenick," *All Things Considered*

✦

"The winds and waves are always on the side of the ablest navigators." – Edward Gibbon, *Decline and Fall of the Roman Empire*

✦

"The bitter and the sweet come from the outside, the hard from within, from one's own efforts." – Albert Einstein, *Out of My Later Years*

✦

"Courage is resistance to fear, mastery of fear – not absence of fear." – Mark Twain, *Pudd'nhead Wilson*

✦

"No one knows what he can do till he tries." – Publilius Syrus, *Moral Sayings*

✦

"Life is filled with suffering, but it is also filled with many wonders, like the blue sky, the sunshine, the eyes of a baby. To suffer is not enough. We must also be in touch with the wonders of life. They are within us and all around us, everywhere, any time." – Thich Nhat Hanh, *Being Peace*

✦

"We are adhering to life now with our last muscle – the heart." – Djuna Barnes, *Nightwood*

╫

APPENDIX B – DEALING WITH RELATIONSHIP STRESS DURING THE BAR EXAM

One major source of stress for people preparing for the bar exam is how their single-minded focus on the bar exam affects their significant other and close family and friends. Because of this, I recommend that you speak with these people early on or ideally before you begin your bar exam preparations.

You should explain that you will be taking the bar exam soon, that it is a difficult test that requires a lot of studying, and that you will not be as available as before. Tell them this will only last a couple of months, but that it will be intense. Promise them (and fulfill that promise!) that you will be available on Saturday and/or Sunday to hang out and that you will be available each day during the evenings to talk. Below are some strategies for speaking with important people in your life.

Significant other

If you have been with your S.O. through law school, then he or she has gotten used to you keeping long hours away in order to attend class, do your homework, study for final exams, and work at clerking gigs. If you have already come to an accommodation about this, then the bar exam should not be much different. Maybe you will be away a couple more hours per day and occasionally on a weekend, but not much more.

If your S.O. is upset at the amount of time you are studying, then assuming you aren't spending more than 50 or 60 hours per week studying (and I don't think you should be) there really is no call for this behavior. Explain that once you get a job as an attorney, it is likely that you will work a minimum of 40 hours per week, which will equate to *at least* 50 hours per week away from home when you factor in lunch breaks, commute time, and extra-curricular, work-related activities. If your S.O. cannot take the time away now, the problem is likely to get worse.

Of course, if you are going to preach in this manner, you have to make sure that the time you do spend with your S.O. is quality time. Vent a little about the bar exam, but do not make it the sole topic of conversation. Study at your study place (e.g., law library) and live the rest of your life when you are at home. (I hate to create some sort of dualistic conflict between life and work, since they are interwoven and cannot really be separated, but it is a useful concept here.)

In the end, if your relationship with your S.O. is healthy going into the bar exam, it should be strong after the bar exam.

Friends

If all of your friends are either in law school or preparing for the bar exam, then there is not much need to have a preemptive talk with them about your coming unavailability. For your friends who are not involved in the legal world, they are probably used to you not being around much during the week because you have been in law school for three years, but your increased unavailability during the evenings and possibly on weekends will be something new.

Therefore, be sure to tell your friends that for the next couple of months, you might not be available to hang out them as much as before. You should encourage them to continue to invite you to go out with them in the evenings because, inevitably, you will want to go out at least a few times during your bar preparations and it would be a shame to miss out on a night with your friends because they think you are too busy. After all, once the bar exam is over, you'll probably want to go out with them for a big blow out celebration, so now is not the time to push them away.

Children

The majority of people taking the bar exam do not have children. For those of you who do, it presents a special problem. If your children are very young (under 3), then the burden is really on whoever will be caring for the children while you are studying. Be sure to thank that person often. If it is your significant other, then get a babysitter every couple of weeks and go out to dinner or even a night away.

If your children are older, then you need to be sure you make time for them. You can tell them you have a very hard test coming up and that you need lots of time alone to study, but many children simply cannot comprehend studying for 8 to 10 weeks straight for a single test. It seems ridiculous to them.

When children are involved, I highly recommend having a set schedule and never varying from it. The importance of having a set schedule is two-fold: (1) your children always know when you are available (e.g., after 5pm M-F, after Noon on Saturday, and all day on Sunday); and (2) you are forced to learn during those hours or else – it is a great motivator

APPENDIX C – HOW TO CREATE YOUR OWN BAR EXAM STUDY SCHEDULE

The basic requirements for creating your own study schedule are simple:

- Know your strengths and weaknesses,
- Set time limits and boundaries, and
- Ensure you review each subject until you learn it.

I will use my study plan for the California bar exam as an example of how to create your own study schedule. The first thing to do is determine exactly what it is the bar examiners of your state will test you on.

The California bar has between 13 and 18 subjects (depending on how you count) from which the bar examiners may draw essay questions. These subjects overlap with the six subjects covered on the MBE. There are also two, three-hour Performance Tests, which require little knowledge of the law, but require practical skills to digest, organize, and write out the information into a coherent and high-scoring answer.

Next, determine how much time you have available to study. Since I had recently relocated to California and was not working, I would be able to study whenever I wanted for the February bar exam. Moreover, since I had recently taken the BarBri lecture course for the Oregon bar and was not about to waste several thousand dollars and 2 hours a day commuting to the BarBri classroom site, I decided to study on my own with the BarBri California books and AdaptiBar for the MBE.

Given all that, I had decided to study from January 7 until February 25 in preparation for the test on February 26, 27, and 28. This is seven weeks of study time, during which I promised myself I would not study on weekends except for the weekend immediately prior to the exam. Thus, studying for seven weeks for 5 days a week gave me 35 days. Now, I could not study at home because it was too distracting. I did not live near a law school, so I could not study at a law library. Any attempt to study at a coffee shop or bookstore is insane (due to the unending external distractions) and should never be attempted. Therefore, I had to study at the local public library.

Because the library did not open until 9:00 a.m., I had an enforced starting point. The library was open until 9:00 p.m. Monday-Thursday, but closed at 5:00 p.m. on Friday. Because I wanted to make each day the same, I promised myself that I would end at 5:00 p.m. or earlier. I used about an hour each day for a 30 minute lunch and some breaks, resulting in 7 hours per day of active study time, or 245 total hours during which I would study for and pass the bar. (If I had been a first-time taker, was studying on my own, and needed to include time to listen to lectures, then I would have needed to add another couple weeks to my schedule or included Saturday as a study day.)

Another bonus to this schedule is that it roughly approximates the hours during which the bar examination is administered. This helps in training the mind and body to be at peak performance during the same hours as the real bar exam occurs.

Now, within these days and hours, I had to prioritize. To prioritize, I needed to assess my strengths and weaknesses. I am a pretty good essay writer, so I knew that I could practice writing comparatively less than the multiple choice questions, which I find quite difficult. On the other hand, the written portions of the California bar exam account for 65% of the final score, so if I were a weak writer, I would focus on that for probably 70% of my study time.

I decided to review two subjects a day until all subjects were covered. From 9:00 a.m. until Noon, I quickly read a BarBri outline in the Conviser Mini Review, then went through it slowly and typed out my own condensed outline, working quickly enough to get it done by Noon. Then, I took a lunch break. After lunch, I did the same thing with the next topic. I made sure that I finished by 4:00 p.m. Then, I went to the California bar website and read as many essays and model answers on each of the day's two topics as I could. When I was too tired or it was 5:00 p.m., I went home.

I cannot emphasize enough the importance of having a concrete ending time to each day of your studies. When I studied for the Oregon bar, my study day was 8:00 a.m., when the BarBri lecture started, to 5:00 p.m. Monday to Friday, and then 10:00 a.m. to 3:00 p.m. on Saturday, and I never studied on Sunday.

You need to set boundaries so that the bar exam does not engulf your life. Part of the Bar Exam Mind philosophy is balance. When you balance your life, your stress naturally goes away (or at least is minimized).

After about 8 days of reviewing two subjects per day, it was time to review my outlines and do practice questions. Again, I would do two topics per day and include 50 or more MBE questions. For instance, I might review community property in the morning and write out 1 or 2 essays. Then after lunch I would review torts and write out 1 or 2 essays. While reviewing each outline, I would also make flash cards for any rule of law that had more than one element (e.g., negligence, burglary, all constitutional law balancing tests, etc.) and for the points of law that seemed difficult for me to remember. Finally, I would do 50 torts questions and then go home.

I repeated this pattern of doing a California-specific topic in the morning and an MBE topic in the afternoon until all 6 MBE subjects were reviewed. Then, I finished up with the remaining California-specific topics and did random MBE questions in the late afternoon. Finally, interspersed within this schedule I had at least one 4-hour block per week where I wrote out a performance test in its entirety and then reviewed the sample answer. (If at all possible, use answers that are passing answers from real bar takers. Your bar preparation program may have such answers. If you are in California, sample essay and performance test answers are posted on the California bar website. These are well-written answers by actual takers.)

Starting about the third week of my studies, I began to create what I call "Issue Pairing" charts. These are charts that allow quick reference to topics that are often tested together.

In my opinion, it is not enough to know that when a Wills question is asked you should go through the elements of a valid formal will. You should also know the esoteric points that the bar examiners are likely to ask about. You learn these by going through sample essays and writing down these issue pairing charts for each topic.

Finally, about two-weeks before the exam, I started to spend more time reviewing the topics that seemed most difficult for me. For instance, because I went to law school in Oregon and never took a community property course, community property was a more difficult topic to review than criminal law. Therefore, I set aside two days during the final two-week period to spend significant periods of time studying community property. Whichever state's bar exam you are taking, you will likely have one or two topics that seem more difficult than the rest.

In summary, know your strengths and weaknesses, set time limits and boundaries, and review each subject until you learn it. Your intuition will help guide you in this. Do not deny, ignore, or discount your intuition as to what is sufficient for you to study.

Know when you have studied enough

As you can see from my account of my study schedule, I packed a lot into each day. The central point is to treat studying like a job: get to work the same time each day, bust ass, and then go home and do something else. The process of studying, like the act of working, should not be constantly present in your life. Make sure your studies become routinized. While routine may not be great for creating inspired ideas, it is superb for enabling skill development and memorization.

What you cannot understand from the account of my study schedule is the fact that some afternoons, my brain was fried. Some days, I literally felt like I could not learn a single additional piece of information; in fact, it felt like I was forgetting things. If this feeling continued for more than about twenty or thirty minutes, I just stopped studying. But, I stayed at the library and did something else: read a book about tomatoes, grabbed a DVD and watched it on my computer, stared out the window. Sometimes, I would be refreshed and feel like studying again; other times, I would just stay at the library until 5pm and then go home. I would not try to make up for this brain freeze by studying later that day. If my brain did not want to study, then it obviously needed a rest.

You also must know when you have studied enough in the larger sense. If you are reviewing your criminal law outline and realize that you know everything in it, then stop reviewing it. Spend the time learning something else. If you are still several weeks out from the bar exam, be sure to go over the criminal law outline once a week instead of two or three times, and keep up the practice criminal MBEs and essays.

What you are hoping to get from studying is a moment of calm where you are at peace with the subject you are studying. If you have ever had this feeling when studying for a college or law school test, then you already know the feeling you are seeking with the bar exam.

APPENDIX D – CONTRACT TO PASS THE BAR

In Chapter Three, I discussed psychologist Robert Chalidi's concept of commitment and consistency. Since you are an aspiring attorney, what better way to implement the principles of commitment and consistency that by entering into a contract with yourself?

In his book, *Influence*, Chaldini recounts the story of how Amway salespeople asked potential customers to fill out their own sales agreements, rather than let the salesperson do it. This greatly increased the number of customers who did not cancel their orders during the "cooling off" periods imposed by state law.

Why not follow Amway's lead and fill out your own contract with yourself to encourage your commitment to study for and pass the bar exam?

Here is a sample contract for your use; replace the italics and blanks with appropriate text, then sign. If you would like an editable version of this contract, please go to **www.barexammind.com/resources** and click on the link that says "Bar Exam Contract." You will be provided with the opportunity to download a rich text format version for your own use.

AGREEMENT TO PASS THE BAR EXAM ADMINISTERED ON *[MONTH] [YEAR]*

The parties to this Agreement are:

1. *[Your name here]*, recent law school graduate; and

2. *[Your name here]*, future attorney at law.

RECEITALS

Whereas the state of _____ offers the bar examination twice per year, in February and July;

Whereas, *[your name here]* has registered to take the bar examination in the state of _____ during *[month] [year]*;

Whereas, both parties agree that passing the bar examination is of great importance;

NOW, THEREFORE, in consideration of the mutual promises and undertakings of the parties hereto, the parties agree as follows:

AGREEMENT

1.   *[Your name here]* promises to study ___ hours per day during the week *[optional: and __ hours per day on the weekend]*.

2.   While studying, *[your name here]* promises to isolate *himself/herself* from all distractions, including email, text messages, social media, and all other electronic distractions as well as noise and other people.

3.   *[Your name here]* promises to use *his/her* best efforts while studying for the bar examination.

4.   *[Your name here]* promises to perform visualizations and affirmations to ensure that *he/she* is confident and prepared when the day of the examination arrives.

5.   *[Your name here]* agrees that *he/she* will eat healthy food, exercise and get enough sleep in order to keep *his/her* body and brain functioning at optimal levels during this strenuous period of study.

6.   Upon receipt of passing results, *[your name here]*, attorney at law, agrees to reward *[your name here]* with *[insert reward that will motivate you]* for *his/her* efforts that resulted in a passing score on the bar exam.

Signed:_____   Signed:_____

[Your name here]   *[Your name here]*

Law School Graduate   Future Attorney at Law

Dated:_____   Dated:_____

⊹

APPENDIX E – MY MELATONIN EXPERIMENT

Melatonin is a hormone made in the brain that helps regulate the body's sleep cycle. Darkness stimulates the production of melatonin while light decreases the production of melatonin. Certain studies have shown that melatonin is effective in decreasing the time required to fall asleep, increasing the number of hours one stays asleep, and improving one's alertness upon waking. Melatonin is recommended to help alleviate symptoms of jet lag. Melatonin is generally considered safe and non-addictive.

In order to see whether melatonin actually works as advertised, I decide to try some on myself. The melatonin that I used was made by a company called Natrol and was in liquid form. The recommended dose was four droppers (4mL) taken 20 minutes before bedtime. Since I had never taken melatonin before, I opted for half the dosage. I took melatonin for three nights in a row, replicating the number of nights before test days during the California bar exam.

Without melatonin, I can generally fall asleep fairly easily, but if I wake up early in the morning (i.e., two or three hours before my normal waking time) I tend to have great difficulty falling back to sleep. Unfortunately, this tends to happen several nights per week. I was interested to see whether the melatonin would affect the speed at which I fall asleep and whether it would help me fall back asleep if I woke up early in the morning.

Night 1

The first night I took melatonin I was amazed at its effect. About 20 to 25 minutes after I took the melatonin, I felt a wave of warmth pass over my body and my muscles seemed to relax. (Note: I have not read anywhere that melatonin acts as a muscle relaxant.) I felt instantly groggy, and a couple minutes later I basically passed out. The next thing I knew, I woke up eight hours later. When I awoke, I felt fully rested without any grogginess that is usually associated with over-the-counter pharmaceutical sleep medications.

Night 2

The second night I took melatonin, I did not experience the wave of warmth that I had felt the first night. I felt groggy, but did not fall asleep instantly like I did the first night. It is possible that the first night I was exceptionally tired and so the melatonin had a more dramatic effect on me. Still, I fell asleep within 30 to 35 minutes of taking the melatonin, and I had a generally restful sleep. I did wake up once at about 3:00 a.m., but was able to fall asleep very quickly, without my mind starting to churn through various thoughts. The next time I woke up was about 20 minutes before my alarm clock would have gone off. I had slept for about seven hours. Again, I had no grogginess in the morning and no ill effects that I could detect.

Night 3

The third night I took melatonin was essentially a repeat of the second night, though I did not wake up early in the morning and slept almost a full eight hours.

Conclusion

Based on my experiment with my own sleeping habits, I believe melatonin does have a beneficial effect on the ability to fall asleep and stay asleep. More importantly for me, I believe using melatonin helps keep the mind calm at night, enabling more restful sleep.

If melatonin sounds like something you might want to use to help you sleep during the bar exam, I suggest you buy some in advance of the bar exam and experiment with it make sure that your mind and body do not have any adverse reaction to it. (Of course, consult your health care provider before using it.)

It should be noted that well-known doctors like Andrew Weil endorse the short-term use of melatonin to reset the body's sleep cycles (such as with jet lag), but do not recommend it for regular use to cure insomnia.

Melatonin is available in liquid or pill form.

╬

ABOUT THE AUTHOR

Matt Racine passed both the Oregon and California bar exams on his first attempt. He credits his success largely to the strategies contained in this book. He currently works as a lawyer in the San Diego area where he practices employment law. He blogs about the bar exam at www.barexammind.com.

Made in the USA
San Bernardino, CA
16 January 2015